"Before enlightenment, chop wood and carry water.

After enlightenment, chop wood and carry water."

—Wu Li

illustrations by
Peter Arkle

TOSKS - see in car
Jive to Kennie
Carnival/Camival/Movies

MINE WORK

NO BITE

85885

THINGS TO BRING, S#!T TO DO

...and other inventories of anxiety

MY LIFE IN LISTS

KAREN RIZZO

Stewart, Tabori & Chang
New York

FOR
Jim,
Drake,
and August,
my inspiration

Chop wood, carry water,
coffee
Powerbars
sunglasses
reading glasses
Advil
graham crackers
sweatshirts
Fruit Gushers
cut apples
jelly beans
cell phone
cell phone # written down
<u>Vanity Fair</u>
<u>Utne</u>
<u>The Gas We Pass</u>
crayons
coloring books
magnetic checkers game
notebook
fine-tip marker
address of where I'm going
karate gi
scooter
skateboard
Barbie in her pink convertible
grocery list
"what to do" list

I make lists. As do most women I know, I make
lists. I make them to free up the disk space in my brain
so that I may be present. Though sometimes I have running
lists in my head so as not to be present. Either way,
I cannot live without making them. Over the years I've
scribbled lists on pads, Post-its, letters, and greeting
cards, in the margins of books, on my kids' artwork, on
my hands, candy wrappers, magazines, broken umbrellas,
disposable diapers, cocktail napkins, toilet paper,
walls, desks, boxes, bags, and sneakers. Some lists are
of what to do, or bring, or buy, or where to go. Some are
inventory of what seemed important on a particular day
or thoughts to muse on later, or of things that I simply
didn't want to forget. Sometimes when I wake early
in the morning, too soon to rise and too late to coax
back sleep, I make lists in my head, just to make sure
that I can remember. Often these lists are more an
inventory of, say, "my favorite hangouts circa 1986," or
"the names of my fifth-grade classmates," or "the
addresses of places I've lived."

Last spring I received an invitation to a baby
shower requesting my presence at a "Wise Woman Circle, at
noon on the Spring Equinox." I hadn't seen the guest of
honor in years and didn't know her friends, but we'd kept
track of each other through the grapevine. I did know
that I would be in the company of women devoted to
disciplined vegan diets and daily yogic rituals—women
who had changed their names to Lakshmi or Shakti (while
keeping surnames the likes of Cohen, Epstein, and
MacDougal)—who were certain to be wearing organic cotton
saris in shades of pumpkin, aquamarine, and rose. As out
of place as I imagined I'd be—lazy, carnivorous, and

jeans-clad as I am—I felt compelled to accept. In lieu of gifts, the guests were asked to bring words of wisdom and experiences as a mother, "whether or not you were a mother of children or, simply, a mothering woman of this planet." Specifically, I was to share "through words, music, or art" my thoughts and knowledge.

Frankly, I was flattered to be included, but completely panicked about the "thoughts and knowledge" part. As I attempted to concoct wise-mother words, all I succeeded in doing was scribbling grocery and to-do lists in the margins of my notepad. What I wound up sharing with the group was a brief collection of twenty years of those lists, which seemed to serve as a blue-print for twenty years of growing up and screwing up, of letting go and letting be, of getting older and, it seemed, a little wiser.

The response I got was generous and surprising. The latter because those lovely women recognized their own right and left turns through life in the lists, and generous because they laughed. It occurred to me how entire lives are recorded in the ongoing, compulsive scribblings of lists. Every day I empty my pockets and bag and car of them. Every woman I know does the same. My parents made lists too—lists on every kind of paper and document, lists that, regretfully, I threw out, deeming them clutter when I sifted through their belongings after their deaths, in search of meaningful references of their lives. It was all there. If only I had known.

As my father lost his memory and drifted into an existence halfway between solid and air, he would make lists aloud to combat his anxiety. He'd name his brothers, all the instruments they once played, places he'd lived, other members of our tiny family—me, my husband, my two kids, my brother and his wife—until he couldn't anymore. It was obviously exhausting, but necessary and life-affirming. My reasons for making lists are not much different.

By the way,
Said to parents at bedtime when I was six
(to ensure that they didn't die before breakfast)

"good night"
"pleasant dreams"
"sleep tight"
"see you in the morning"
"we'll have breakfast together"
"you, too, whatever you say"
"don't forget your seatbelts"
"sack o' potatoes"
"adios, amigos" (added at age seven)

My favorite hangouts...NYC, 1986

Jimmy Ray's
Film Center Café
McHales
Possible 20's
Arriba Arriba
West Bank Cafe
Marvin's

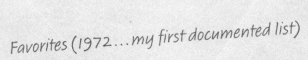

Favorites (1972... my first documented list)

song: <u>Song Sung Blue</u>

color: purple

person: Mom

place: New York City

friends: Meggy Friedman, Caren Levy

food: Salisbury steak TV dinner, Shar Shu Ding, shrimp toast, McDonald's double cheeseburger, olives from Dad's martini, peaches

TV show: <u>The Wonderful World of Disney</u>

jewelry: amethyst ring Mom bought me at Fortunoff's

animal: horse

book: <u>Are You There, God? It's Me, Margaret</u>

Here is a pen and here is a pencil,
Here's a typewriter, here's a stencil,
Here is a list of today's appointments,
And all the flies in all the ointments,
The daily woes that a man endures –
Take them, George, they're yours!

—Ogden Nash

Father's Day 1982

<u>Bring to hospital</u>

Lox and bagels [Mom is on her first day of recovery
   from a radical mastectomy and she wants bagels from
   Bagel City and lox from Sheppy's—enough for the
   entire nursing staff and all her breastless comrades
   on the floor. "Are you resting?" My father asks over
   the phone as I listen in. "Rest shmest," she says.
   "I got naps coming outta my ears and it looks like a
   goddamned morgue in here. Honey, you'll take some
   flowers home when you leave." Mom continues on about
   the "dynamite gal" down the hall with the double
   mastectomy and Pucci scarves wrapping up her bald head.
   "Happy Father's Day, Rizzo," she says finally. "And
   pick up a pound of sturgeon."]

new flannel nightgown

<u>TV Guide</u>

<u>People</u> magazine

Norman Cousins book

Fresca, butterscotch candy, pears, Jarlsberg cheese

pink nail polish

Silly String

Bring to beach (August 1982)

August 1982

<u>Bring to beach</u>

baby oil
pot, pipe, matches
blanket
boom box
<u>Mademoiselle</u>, <u>Esquire</u>
M&Ms, potato chips
Diet Pepsi
bad-tasting nail stuff

July 1983

<u>Today</u>

planetarium?

shopping with Mom [for a new prosthetic boob, because
    she's thrown the old one across the room one too many
    times. She hit me in the back of the head with the
    thing, trying to get my attention while I was watching
    <u>60 Minutes</u>. It bounced off me and hit Mike Wallace in
    the face, at which point my mother laughed too hard.
    I picked it up, a flesh-colored flat-backed beanbag
    with a nipple, and thought of that carnival game in
    which you try to toss a beanbag into a hole for a
    prize. They ought to use <u>these</u> things—more adults
    would play. More kids, too. No, maybe not.
        That night I thought I heard my mother crying in

the shower. "Mom? Ma?"

"Can't a person shower in peace?" she yelled back through the door. "Now go ask your father what he wants for dinner."]

clean out closets

call B [and tell him that he's not even human, that he's an amoeba. And ask someone else to go to the Squeeze concert with me. And don't date guys with reality-impaired ex-girlfriends who ice-pick my tires.]

<u>Notorious</u> at St. Mark's

writing class

buy <u>Fool for Love</u> tickets

no white flour, sugar

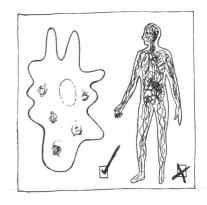

August 1983

<u>I must read</u>

<u>The Iliad</u>, Homer
<u>Civilization and Its Discontents</u>, Freud
<u>Don Quixote</u>, Cervantes
<u>Crime and Punishment</u>, Dostoyevsky
<u>Inferno</u>, Dante
<u>Remembrance of Things Past</u>, Proust

September 1983

To do

Rosh Hashanah at Aunt Jessie's?

pick up Chinese

get work schedule [I'm one of two token Caucasian
  waitresses in a Japanese restaurant. The owner is an
  ex-garmento with impeccable taste in jewelry, manicured
  fingernails, and a wife with chronic shiny chin from
  devouring fatty tuna sashimi between seatings. The rest
  of the staff is the size and weight of my left leg.
  There is barely room in the kitchen for me to scoop
  rice without knocking out the eighty-pound tempura
  chef. I got stoned with one of the waiters. He told
  jokes in fractured English and the punchlines in
  Japanese. I kept thinking that I knew Japanese.
  I don't. I'm giving up pot.]

fitting for R's bridesmaid dress

date with S?

get a perm

March 1984

sell car

Carumbas! w/ Sasha [This time we will stop drinking before she takes off her shirt and pretends to be a jet plane careening down Eighth Avenue.]

tckts for <u>Glengarry Glen Ross</u>

buy cardboard closet [for my very own closetless, view-impaired apartment in Hell's Kitchen.]

hooks

roach traps and spray

carpet cleaner, Drano

interview roommates

DO NOT DATE CUTE ACTORS WHO DON'T KNOW THEY'RE GAY

Fran Lebowitz, Sam Shepard—bookstore!

Hitchcock fest?

find new acting class [I cannot do another improv with the instructions "You are living in a trailer park and have a baby with spina bifida. Your lying, cheating husband has just walked in from an all-night orgy. Now begin the scene ... "]

November 1984

find new aerobics class [because the one I took last
   week, my first ever, caused me to throw up, and then
   sleep for twenty-four hours. Must I grind my body to a
   Eurythmics soundtrack in order to atone for years of
   impersonating a sloth?]

fast

buy pineapples [for after fast. Stop eating them before
   tongue bleeds.]

doc appointment [What are symptoms of an ulcer?]

talk to S [Assure her that she can date What's-his-face
   because I have, indeed, broken up with him. Warn her
   not to attend any weddings with him at Kiwanis Clubs,
   as she may, as I did, get in the middle of a fistfight
   between bridesmaids. Personally, I have never seen pink
   taffeta move so fast and so hard. My black Qiana dress
   has a run in it from the armpit to the ankle. Serves
   me right for dating someone who's trying to impersonate
   Ernest Hemingway.]

hair appt. [to CUT OFF PERM]

jog...three-mile loop! [A jogging man collapsed in front
   of my house when I was fifteen. My mother was looking
   out the window at exactly that moment and called to my
   father, who ran across the street with a blanket,
   covered the man, and sat beside him as Mom called 911.
   A couple of days later she called hospitals trying

to find out about the man. He was dead when he hit
the curb, that middle-aged man in the red sweatbands
and running suit, she was told. Nothing anyone could
have done. She finagled his name and number and
called his wife just to let her know that her husband
had not died alone, that there were people who cared
by him in the end. My mother thinks that jogging is
ridiculous for anyone over thirty. I assure her that
I will quit long before then. She'll see.]

January 1985

Groceries (single)

Ben & Jerry's Cherry Garcia
Rolling Rock beer
peanut butter
celery
dijon mustard
popcorn
Folgers instant coffee
Marlboro Lights

March 1985

rehearsal schedule? [I'm part of an experimental theater
    piece downtown and have to gouge out my eyes, drip
    blood through the audience, then break my mirror image
    into a hundred shards of glass. Playing opposite me is

a world-weary-at-twenty-five leather-clad actor with a dog-eared copy of <u>Portrait of the Artist as a Young Man</u> in his back pocket, yearning to play Stanley in <u>Streetcar</u>, who arrives late to rehearsals because he's always "just had the best fucking sex" with his girl-friend. The other woman in the piece is a delicate, Irish redhead who speaks in a shittin' Irish accent as in "you're shittin' me, you fuckin' shit. Shit, that just shits," and thinks I'm a loser because I wear a hat and scarf. My aunt Jessie, a therapist, thinks I would make a good shrink. That's nice. And then Stanley and Red could be my first clients.]

call landlord re: ROACHES!

THE SMITHS!

Call L—pick me up after the play tomorrow [I can't help but be charmed by him. He drives an Italian sports car that he had converted to automatic transmission because, admittedly, he couldn't drive, smoke, and drink coffee at the same time. He showed up for lunch where I work five days in a row then finally asked my name. I thought he asked what the soup of the day was. "Chicken noodle," I said. So now we are dating.]

call Mom

leave note for A [My roommate. Let her know I'm coming home early tonight, lest I walk in on another emotional, seminude, scene rehearsal for her method acting class.]

put trampoline on street [That would be the five-foot-
   wide personal workout trampoline that's taking up my
   entire bedroom. I bought it two months ago because
   I couldn't afford Jack La Lanne, which isn't a problem
   now that I have a credit card. I'll miss bouncing up
   and down to an old Devo album, leg weights strapped to
   my ankles and wrists, no matter how mortified I would
   have been to have someone actually see me doing it.
   I won't miss the afternoon I had to carry the leaden
   thing home in a giant square box, up Sixth Avenue, in
   a gale force Arcticdraft. It was like maneuvering some
   insane Lockheed-made moon kite between my fists. After
   being blown over in front of Rock Center, I tried to
   hail a cab, in rush hour, eyes stinging from the wind
   and the utter frustration of having not one person
   pause to give me a hand. I wanted to toss it under-
   neath an uptown bus and call Mom. "Mom, help. Mom, what
   do I do?" But Mom was in the hospital again and, at
   this point, I'd better get used to hauling trampolines
   by myself for the rest of my life.]

July 1985

go to gym

tckts for the Public

find out what happened to Mike [I heard he sold coke to
   the wrong person and was fired. He used to toss around
   cocaine-stuffed cigarettes at Danceteria. Now he is
   gone. Poof. As are Eddy and DL. Cocaine. DL was buying

the stuff from some guy at the park on Tenth Avenue.
Didn't he see the car full of burly undercover
cops dressed as if they were going deer hunting? You
couldn't help but notice them on the way to the Korean
market—a bunch of white guys in plaid flannel shirts
and caps crammed into a Plymouth in Hell's Kitchen on
a rainy afternoon. Not everyone can be Serpico.]

Note to Miguel [Who has had a "cold" for six weeks.
Another waiter at the restaurant died. His boyfriend is
sick too. JD says that his roommate has some mysterious
illness that he "got from traveling in a car with a
constant draft on his neck.'" Mm-hmm. Steven and Michael
are well. They're in their thirties and have been
together "forever." I will join them with ML for a
cocktail and high tea, and they'll talk about theater,
movies, how glad they are for having "sown their wild
oats a million years ago," and tell me how much I
resemble some 1940s Latina movie diva named Maria
Montez. After a few toddies we will go to a piano bar
and I will actually become Maria.]

pick up cigarettes and chips

temp agency typing test

call landlord re: toilet [I may have dropped an eyeliner
in it. Maybe don't tell him that.]

September 1985

<u>I want</u>

a paying acting job

to quit my waitressing job

to meet someone who doesn't talk about himself,
    his ex-girlfriend, how his mother fucked him up,
    or his workout routine

to move objects with my mind

an apartment without a roommate

a roommate who isn't crazy

everyone to stop talking about Shakti Gawain

to not sit next to someone chanting "Nam-myoho-renge-kyo"
    on the A train.

December 1985

<u>I know</u>

I will be on Johnny Carson's <u>Tonight Show</u> one day. I will
    tell Johnny that my epitaph will be, "She had a rye
    sense of humor in a pumpernickel world." He will laugh
    and say that is the best epitaph he has ever heard.

I will guest-host more often than Joan Rivers.

Leslie would tell MF to fuck off (if she was me)

I wish I had written <u>Prizzi's Honor</u>

Elephants use a secret language of low-frequency sounds,
  inaudible to humans, to communicate with other members
  of a herd

My parents are still in love

March 1986, 3:30 A.M.

<u>Ask Mom. Soon. Maybe.</u>

Why didn't you want to bring me and Ken up Jewish?
  Why didn't you bring us up <u>something</u>?

Do you believe in God?

Please tell me why you listened to the doctor who
  suggested that you "watch" a lump in your breast for
  a year, until it was the size of a golf ball, before
  doing anything about it? And do you want me to track
  down and beat up said doctor? [Dr. Gyno Denial, is now
  MIA. A parade of former patients, done with "watching"
  their lumps to "see what happens," are pursuing law-
  suits against him as they finalize last wills and
  requests. Note to self: Question everything. Question
  everyone. Never not question.]

When were you happiest?

What town in Russia was your father from?

How can you and Dad afford to go to Hawaii?

You've beaten this thing, haven't you?

June 1986

DO IT

memorize second act [of play I've been cast in by woman
with an Upper West Side/summers in Italy/Yale pedigree
who peppers her direction with references to Chekhov,
Sartre, and the Cowboy Junkies, then checks to see
if my face is a blank. I want to say, "I don't give
a shit about the Cowboy Junkies; did a paper on The
Cherry Orchard and a production of No Exit. Fuck you."
Instead I nod. I can't stand her, and it's the kind of
can't stand that translates into "I wish I were her."
So fuck you, I want to be you, the realization of
which embarrasses me immensely, so I smile and nod
even more furiously.]

buy bathing suit [for water-skiing date with Michael,
nice boy with a corporate job and a motorboat. Do I
water-ski? "Yes, well, briefly, sort of, at summer
camp," I say.
    "Summer camp! Best times of my life were at summer
camp! Yeah!" Oh, yeah? Well, not me, too. Camp Mohican

was where I went—a Jewish sleepaway camp for certain Brooklyn, Queens, and Long Island neighborhoods. Mom put it on a credit card (she was _so_ way ahead of her time in credit-card debt) and sent my brother and me off with her fond memories of a precious two weeks spent at Girl Scout camp one summer—the happiest two weeks of her childhood—sitting around a campfire, arm in arm with her sister Scouts, singing songs about fishes and friendship.

You couldn't miss me on the archery field at Mohican. I was the skinny one in blue polyester gym shorts and matching polo shirt, trying not to have the worst summer of her life. My bunkmates were the girls in halter tops, Huk-A-Poo shirts, and ripped denim cutoffs. I was also the only person (aside from my brother) whose last name ended in a vowel. "What's your de-al?" Laurie Levine would whine.

"Well, my mother's Jewish and my father's Ital—"

"Ugh," she'd say, as she spat a freshly chewed toe-nail out of her mouth. What was that 'ugh' for? The toenail? My half-Jewishness? My transparent cheerful demeanor in the hope to not be tortured by her and her friends for the rest of the summer?

"My buds and I spend every weekend on the lake. With the girlfriends. It's a big party, like college," Michael told me. Okay. Maybe I'll ask to be scheduled at work on the weekends after all.]

coffee with Stan? [At the CPA firm where I'm temping, Stan, the boss's nephew, a fledgling accountant in a short-sleeved dress shirt, stands in my periphery try-ing to think of how to ask me to lunch. I can tell that's what he wants because he has nothing to do in

Bring to beach (August 1986)

that particular corner of the room and has told me
three times today what a good job his uncle thinks I'm
doing. His uncle doesn't know who I am. I think if
I stood on my desk, pulled my skirt over my head, and
lit a match under the sprinklers, Stan would still be
standing there, telling me what a good job I'm doing.]

Dean & Deluca

condolence card to Tim's boyfriend

Sergio Leone fest—Film Forum?

call SM re: HIV test

August 1986

Bring to beach

running shoes

hand weights

leg weights

Walkman

sunscreen

water

pineapple

Dexatrim [Does anyone else remember how manic and short-
    tempered our mothers were for a couple years in the
    mid 1970s? Think about it now, the bottle of tiny
    prescription pills in the kitchen cabinet between the
    St. Joseph and the Bufferin. Think about it, Mom
    shrinking a couple sizes too quickly from that healthy,
    stout size fourteen. Those first- and second-generation
    mothers with sturdy names like Bea and Flo, Mary,
    Esther, Bernice, and Norma, whose parents and grand-
    parents came from Poland, Russia, Italy, and
    Ireland. ... Go east, young women, to the promised land
    of the Island—suburban Long Island. Go east and wear
    lime-green polyester pantsuits and velvet muumuus and
    trust your doctor to give you a little something for
    that perpetual fifteen-pound excess.]

November 1986

call Leslie and Sam [Ivan is born, so they are parents
    now. I may wait to visit them until Ivan can talk.
    What do I bring? A stuffed bear, right? I don't much
    know what to make of babies. Never known or held one;
    can't remember my brother Ken or me as one. Don't imag-
    ine myself as a mother. Wonder if my mother imagined
    herself as one before she was.]

take Mom shopping [She can no longer drive and it's the
    milestone in her illness that's hardest for her to
    bear. But she tells me that she has potential to be

"a kick-ass talent agent" in her next career, after
she "beats this fartin' thing."

My mother sees the potential in people. Her occasional and tiny real estate office staff always
reflected that: Sandi, with the indecipherable Bronx
accent, layers of makeup and metallic blue shadow
who'd begged her husband to let her work and who,
in my mother's words, was a "sharp gal with great
potential as soon as I can get her to scrape off some
of that pancake." There was the young divorcée with
three teens and an abusive ex-husband, who came to
work for Mom—"a smart cookie with terrific promise
once we get her out from under that lousy shit of an
ex-husband." Another woman, devoutly Catholic and
conservative, who'd decided that she needed to venture
out into the world since her kids were in school.
She'd never even sold a Girl Scout cookie or uttered
an expletive worse than "fudge." In my mother's
estimation, she was a lovely gal who just needed to
"get over the 'fudge' routine and get her ass in gear."

Mom wants a bright cotton blouse so maybe she
"won't look like crap."]

date with D?

make plans with Sasha

work out

memorize scene

talk with Ken [When's the band's next gig? Why are all
   your girlfriends refugees from an Eastern bloc?

Let's go see a play. What will happen to Dad?]

Thanksgiving where?

leftover shrimp salad [Take it home from work.]

December 1986

Christmas gifts

scarf [for Mom]

pin [for Barbara]

hat [for Dad]

1964 World's Fair cufflinks [for Ken]

greeting cards [I am so broke. So pathetically,
    embarrassingly, annoyingly fucking broke. I've been
    fired from my waitressing job for giving away piña
    coladas to my friends at happy hour. I am pathetic.
    That bar is pathetic. My friends are pathetic for
    drinking piña coladas and eating shitty, cold, faux
    Chinese noodles at 5:00 in the afternoon. We are all
    stupid. We need to get real lives. My mother will
    die soon, and when she reaches wherever and is
    questioned by whomever, she will say, "I loved my
    daughter dearly and I know she loved me and it doesn't
    matter that she waited tables at a shitty bar in
    Manhattan." Maybe Ken will go out for cheap happy

hour drinks with me and cry. We'll get drunk and go
dancing at Heartbreaks.]

stop biting nails

get master's degree

get up early

take vitamins

write in journal

gym three times a week!

learn Italian

visit Mom [and if I happen to bump into Mom's best
friend at Penn Station again, this time I will be sure
to tell her that cancer is not contagious and that
if she doesn't contact Mom soon she will have to do it
via séance.]

January 16, 1987

get a fucking haircut

use moisturizer

buy cigarettes

pay bills

fuck the master's degree

lunch with Joan [Lately she's taken to pointing out gaunt
    young men on the street walking with canes, looking
    like they're a hundred years old. They wear long over-
    coats with scarves and hats, and Joan sighs all the way
    to the coffee shop, knocking her knuckles to her heart
    when she sees them.]

visit Mom

February 17, 1987

tell someone it's my birthday

call Dad

write letter to editor about stupid
    New York Times piece by arrogant literary shmuck

meet D for dinner

tulips for Mom

Penn Station at 9:45

kill the sixth person who hassles me for change

March 11, 1987

write note to BR about Mom's eulogy [And ask for a copy.]

call Aunt Jessie, Aunt Charlotte

thank rabbi

thank you's to friends

call Leslie, Todd

call Newsday re: Mom's obituary [Lie about her date of birth. Mom would've appreciated that.]

look for old phone message tapes!

EM [Call and tell her what a fucking idiot she is for leaving an hour-long stream-of-consciousness monologue about NOTHING on my message machine ERASING OVER every remaining message from my MOTHER because she talked till the end of the fucking cassette tape. No, I shouldn't call her. I should just go over there and kill her. I now have no recording of Mom's voice. Maybe Aunt Jessie has some old 8mm footage with Mom on it.]

Dad. What about Dad?

Mom's clothes?

April 1987

<u>Do it</u>

bring stuff to D's apartment [I'm moving in with him.
See, my lease is up and I have a sinus infection that's
draining fluorescent fluids from my skull, colors the
likes of which do not normally appear in nature. D is
sexy and hands take-out to homeless people late at
night. He doesn't ask me hard questions like What do
I <u>really</u> think, Where am I going, or Where have I
been, and he thinks I'm <u>complicated</u>. We do dinner and
Schwarzenegger and Bruce Willis movies. I go to foreign
ones by myself and meet my friends late at night.
This will be good.]

weekend with Dad—toss ALL morphine, syringes, pills

note to Mom's doctor [Thanks for coming to the house a
few weeks back, even though in between your trip from
Mom's bedside to the backyard to steal a smoke, you
told me that I should seriously consider having kids in
my twenties. Something about cancer odds, you said.
Yes, I'll get right on that.]

ACT UP fund-raiser tickets

Dad re: grief group? [He'll never go.]

August 1987

<u>To do</u>

lose six pounds

go to the gym

see <u>Suspicion</u> downtown

make dentist appointment

find lucrative, rewarding career

write novel

buy lottery tickets

move (or join Peace Corps)

call Ken [How are you doing? I've been going to the phone
    to call Mom. While I'm listening to the dial tone, I
    <u>remember</u>. Then I say, "Mom?" aloud anyway, just to hear
    how it used to sound from my mouth. "Mom. Mother. Ma."]

December 1987

Do it

get fake nails

buy batteries

finish Night [then NO MORE Holocaust books]

save New York Times "God on the Answering Machine"

apply for credit card(s)

run FAST

quit yoga class

no refined sugar

March 1988

Do

quit job [because I can't serve another shot of Sex on
   the Beach to a group of Mafia sons out on the town,
   drunk pro-ball players, wrestler boys from local
   colleges, or the heat-seeking bombshell ex-wives of
   famous athletes. It's also somewhat inappropriate for
   bouncers to punch out drunken loudmouths in a way that
   said loudmouths cannot get up from the pavement and
   must be carted off horizontally in neck braces by
   city employees.]

look into therapy [because I'm still crying on buses
   and subways, thinking about all the things I should and
   could have said to Mom before she was too weak to
   listen and the shadow spiders crowded her brain. She
   shouldn't have been such...such...such a grown-up.
   She should have cried long and hard and out loud where
   I <u>could</u> <u>hear</u>. She should have admitted she was scared.
   I should have admitted that I was scared. Still, I
   aspire to her spirited denial, her resilience and
   discretion. But why don't we learn about death while in
   life? Do you miss the smell of rain and peaches after
   you die? I need some answers.]

change rehearsal schedule

finish story for class

go to gym

watch <u>Babette's Feast</u>

apply at E's restaurant

meet Dad at Penn Station [He's the sixty-something guy
   who'll be dashing up the stairs in his signature dark
   Ray-Bans and beige sports jacket. We'll hop in a cab
   and go down to CBGB, a dark, dank club downtown where
   you have to step over needles and sleeping bums to get
   to the entrance, to see my brother's band. Dad will
   sit, as he does, at a table with me and my friends and
   manage to get a smile out of the grim, punked-out wait-
   ress. Afterward, he'll go up to the stage to shake
   hands with the band and tell them, as always, "Great

show. You guys are terrific. I'd just like to hear the lyrics better." He'll look on proudly as the boys pack up their equipment amidst frenzied conversations and thundering speakers.]

November 1988

Do

gym

finish play

eat vegetarian

call unemployment office [And why, Ms. Rizzo, do you qualify? Well, because the paranoid, coke-addled owner of my former place of employment was eavesdropping, as he tended to, on one of my phone conversations. I heard him pick up the phone but continued talking.

    Me: So, is it a deal, then? Are they interested?

    My brother: They're totally into it, but we haven't talked money yet.

    Click.

    That referring to a possible record contract for Ken's band. My psychopathic alien-abductee employer thought I was talking about a drug deal. He fired me that night, on the grounds that I didn't look happy enough taking orders for a round of beef burritos. That is why I qualify.]

meet D's ex-girlfriend [who is in town and is still good
    friends with my boyfriend. How wonderful and civilized
    that I have such a wonderful and civilized boyfriend
    that he can be close with his ex-girlfriends.
        He: I'm friends with all my exes.
        Me: Really?
        He: We're still close.
        Me: Hmmm.
        He: You're not in touch with...?
        Me: No, they're dead.
        He: What? All of them?
        Me: Yes. I killed them when we broke up.]

call and thank JB [for referring me to Big TV Comedy
    Producer after seeing the play I wrote. Too bad Big TV
    Comedy Producer brought me in for a "casual chat," then
    proceeded to call in all her comedy writers and demand
    that I be funny. Also too bad that I lack the ability
    to think clearly under pressure and did my entire show
    in triple-time without breathing in the middle of a
    circle of people taking notes. I wanted to pass out,
    but there wasn't enough room to fall without gouging my
    eye out on a knee. But I will be gracious. Thank you.
    Thank you for an opportunity that ended in my needing
    to vomit.]

ease up on caffeine

January 1, 1989

<u>Do</u>

visit Ken [who is in the hospital with a shard of glass
   in his thigh from a champagne goblet. He finally
   checked himself in after his leg swelled to twice its
   normal size. A doctor said that he was one step away
   from a blood clot traveling up to his brain and killing
   him. Bring Chinese food and a Heineken.]

call Dad [Make sure that the blowzy German lady with
   the cotton-candy hair didn't follow him home. I took
   my father to a New Year's Eve party thrown by my
   boyfriend's mother. At ten of midnight I found him in
   the kitchen hiding from the large fifty-something woman
   in the hot-pink dress wrapped around her body like
   sausage casing, who'd been following him around,
   breathing into his ear. My father was standing with his
   Scotch, looking as if he'd seen a man-eating ghost,
   hiding from Inga. Inga the former actress who'd once
   boffed Bob Crane. "Poor, man, but a lot of fun,"
   she told us before turning her sights on my father.
      I escorted Dad to the lobby and hailed him a taxi
   to Penn Station. Inga was right behind us and jumped in
   the cab before anyone could speak. As they pulled away,
   my father turned around, looking like a man who had
   just been dropped in a crate with a python and tossed
   to sea. I laughed out loud in the lobby as the clock
   struck midnight.]

brunch with P

clean out closet

run at reservoir

finish essay

no sugar

no nail biting

June 1989

<u>Today</u>

pack for workshop!

Niagaras at Continental Divide

application—bartending gig—tux?

deadly South American bugs?

fix Mom's watch [even though it will cost a fortune.
  Then wear it.]

get copies of trip pics [although I look seriously
  depressed even in the ones I'm smiling in. D believes
  we had a great time and left a deposit for next year.
  Next year? If there's a next year there'll be some
  great black-and-whites of me tying rocks to my ankles
  and wading into the lake with a bottle of tequila.

Thinking about "that young blond Jim," as Leslie refers
to him, with the baggy low-slung jeans...Who dresses
like that? None of the guys wearing pants-like-pigskin-
over-footballs that I know. I thought he was fat when
he first came into Leslie's all-women writing class—my
class. The other women knew better immediately. One
whispered loudly about pulling those baggy Levi's down
to his ankles. I saw him in that play in the spring.
He came onstage for one good, long monologue, then made
his exit. I remember nothing else about the play or the
other actors or that evening. We are meeting for coffee
on Thursday.]

End of August 1989

coffee with Jim [I'll test him by suggesting he hook up
   with the pretty cherub-faced blond who stares at him in
   class. I'll tell him that I'm thinking of moving to
   Chicago. I'll ask him if he's dating. He's not dating.
   I'd know if he was dating. I'll just ask him if he
   wants to double-date with me and my boyfriend. He'll
   seriously think I'm a jerk.]

Niagaras at China Club?

call Dad re: what time here?

Liz cover my shift?

learn harmonica

EMT training?

DO REWRITES BY NOON or be an asshole

move to Chicago? [I've been trying to imagine myself in
   forty years with D, on an old porch, surrounded by our
   kids and grandkids, but my brain goes white and the
   reception fails.]

dry cleaner

stop kidding self

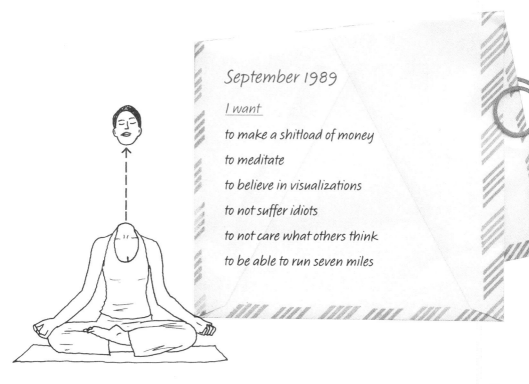

September 1989

<u>I want</u>

to make a shitload of money

to meditate

to believe in visualizations

to not suffer idiots

to not care what others think

to be able to run seven miles

October 1989

To do

run five miles today!

sign up for writing class

buy new jeans

new black Reebok sneaks

toss everything with shoulder pads

Ivan's birthday... superhero... bugs? [He is three and I'm
    his birthday date. He is round and funny and demanding
    and has twenty-seven hundred action figures and eighty-
    seven Barbies. I just want to get him a present that
    he doesn't have and will like better than anyone
    else's. Listen to me. I'm five.]

clean out closet

dinner with Dad

Prickasaurus——at Shrieber Studios

tell D I must move out [If he's angry or dismayed, I
    don't imagine he'll show it. I do imagine that he'll
    wish me "an easeful, peaceful life," the best in
    all my future endeavors, and watch me leave through
    a haze of Nag Champa incense from his headstand in a
    corner of the room.]

January 1990

Pack!

call Danny re: van?

desk to Ken

cycle jacket—where is it?

get bed from Kathy?

is Rod sick?

Jim re: dinner at my place
  [where I am moving to this afternoon.]

February 1990

<u>Do</u>

Thank you to agent [for calling me in because he liked
me in "that little play... what was it called?" and I
had "some young Anjelica Huston thing going on," but
I'm too "offbeat," and I should get my teeth filed and
dress sexier. So, thank you for letting me sit in your
office while you kvelled for twenty minutes on the
phone over a Michelle Pfeiffer look-alike that you discovered in a student scene-night, and for giving me
your sublime insights as to why Melanie Griffith is a
star. And thanks for my ripped $10 pantyhose and the
$15 cab it took to make it there on time, and for my
missed work shift. Thanks.

　　See, my friend Jordan calls these "letters never

to be sent." But it's important to write them and drop them without addresses into mail boxes so as to "let go." I'm letting go. I'm seeing you in my morning meditation swathed in blue light, floating above me, smiling... I feel the love... and acceptance... and then you explode into a million pieces to the cheering throngs of a packed Yankee Stadium.]

get to yoga class

run

clean out closet

condolence card to M

prep tax stuff

Shambala workshop? [IamawarriorIamawarriorIamawarrior.]

eat some fucking vegetables

March 1990

<u>Do</u>

quit job [But I won't, as I am being paid good money
as a research drone at a small PR firm. Although I did
work very hard on that Valentine's Day campaign for
<u>H</u> magazine, finding how to say "I love you" in twenty-
seven different languages. Got the Serbo-Croatian
phrase wrong and had to get on the phone with the
Serbian embassy while my supervisor stood over me,
spitting obscenities. What I'd like to do is scream
back at her. No, better yet, what I'd like to do
is turn to her and belt out "Fly Me to the Moon" the
next time she chews me out, or "Color My World,"
which, according to the hundred AM DJs I queried
across the country for same Valentine's campaign, is
<u>the</u> romantic song of choice. What year is it anyway?]

stop biting nails

get bad-tasting nail stuff

rent <u>Stalag 17</u> and <u>Sweet Smell of Success</u>

pint Cherry Garcia

finish rewrites

tickets for <u>The Grapes of Wrath</u>

September 1990

<u>Buy</u>

shoes for bridesmaid dress [What to wear with a pink
  ballet tutu designed with the adult anorexic in mind?
  Unfortunately, I am the wrong shape and have never
  uttered the word "tulle" until now.]

gift for Sasha

lottery tickets

clothes for camping trip [My first ever. Me—a girl who
  never slept outside or saw an animal without a collar
  that wasn't at the Bronx Zoo, whose parents' idea of a
  hike was driving to a faraway diner in search of the
  perfect breakfast danish—with Jim, outdoors boy who
  climbed things, speared fish in streams, and had neigh-
  bors who killed their own food.
    What to wear? One would wear camping pants to camp.
  I'll go to Banana Republic and buy camping pants and
  a pith helmet and wear my red ropers. Jim is going to
  get me real hiking boots. Okay, what are they and do
  they hurt? It will be fun, camping. Sure. An adventure.
  No porcelain or hot water? I'm going to be constipated
  for a week.]

suitcase for camping

first-aid kit

white T-shirts [Right? For camping?]

sunscreen

warm clothes,
    nice underwear

Learn (January 1991)

- Italian

- harmonica

- guitar

- tai chi

- how to ski

- how to make $3,000 a week
              in my spare time

February 1991

Today!

beet-and-parsley juice to M
    [She is kicking heroin. Also bring B vitamins and
    protein powder.]

see ophthalmologist? [Sometimes out of the corner of
    my eye I think I see small animal shadows skitter
    across the floor. Maybe not an ophthalmologist, maybe
    a psychic.]

new workout clothes [Jim made fun of my metallic blue
    spandex tights and matching leotard. I can't get angry
    at him because he made me laugh at the same time...
    and he's going bald at twenty-six.]

get Bottom Line tickets—Tanya coming?

switch shifts w/ Tina

Jim re: what time at Grand Central [My birthday. Jim is
taking me somewhere for the weekend. It's a surprise.
He doesn't pull the "So what do you want to do/what'd
you have in mind/what do you feel like for your
birthday?" routine. He just does. He has planned
everything, telling me simply to dress warmly and
forget about phones.
    He is relentless in wanting to know what I think,
what I dream, how I feel. He will not let me fly
on automatic pilot for an instant. My song and dance
doesn't work. Thank God.]

February 1992

Before moving [into a Brooklyn apartment with Jim]

quick run

call Marc and Suz [They and Joe, our good and lovely
friends, are moving us. We will pay them in falafel and
cheap wine.]

call Joe—tell him to eat [before he helps to move us,
otherwise we'll have to stop the van in midtown for
a slice.]

find Richard Thompson CD; Velvet Underground and Stevie
Ray Vaughan tapes

pack up last shelf

leave note for K

pick up U-Haul [and trust that our future landlord, the
man in the silk smoking robe—with the crazy tufts of
white hair, wielding a brandy snifter, playing <u>Aida</u> at
200 decibels, who greeted us at his Brooklyn brownstone
six weeks ago to this day—was not a figment of our
frozen imaginations. Abel, his name was—is...we hope.
Jim and I had knocked on his front door by accident.
But he invited us in, the two wind-whipped strangers in
black leather, with scarves wrapped around runny noses,
clutching the "For Rent" sections of three newspapers.
    He said that he wasn't planning on renting his
garden apartment, but showed it to us anyway—an apartment packed with the musty artifacts of his recently
deceased and very much missed anthropologist wife.
There was a hole in the ceiling the size of a bowling
ball, and little room to make it from one end of the
place to the other, but light found its way through
the window to the floors, which were beautiful oak.
And then there was the garden. A real garden. He asked
us what we could pay and we told him. He said to come
back today, without even asking our last names or
numbers. And I half-imagine that we'll return to that
address and there'll be a huge hole in the ground,
and Jim and I will realize that we both manifested the
same <u>Brigadoon</u> garden apartment.]

Bring to beach (August 1992)

August 1992

<u>Bring to beach</u>

sunscreen, lipstick, cover stick
beer, water
blanket
chips
peaches
Walkman
<u>Vanity Fair</u>

December 1992

<u>December stuff!</u>

homemade Kahlúa recipe?

Look for bottles—Sixth Avenue flea market

jambalaya?

lard—where? yuck

talk to Marc, Suz, Joe, Frank—guitars, dinner

gifts for Jim and Sherrie [Jim and Sherrie, Jim's dad
    and stepmom. Jim 'n' Sher, impossibly sane and satis-
    fied people, despite having brought together four
    wildly different kids from two marriages. They live on
    the Florida gulf coast and like Miller Lite, Regis

and Kathie Lee, romantic comedies, Jimmy Buffett,
rollerblading, and jogging on the beach. Jogging.
What would Mom say?]

January 1993

Pack for road trip to LA [where Jim and I are going for a
three-month visit, and Jim will get a TV series and
I... I will... I will change my name to Charlene and
join the rodeo circuit, singing country music ballads
in between bronco rides.]

typewriter

photos

stories, play, screenplay

summer clothes

trip music

interview skirt/jacket

X-mas gift for Greg [Jim's younger brother, whose place
in Tucson we will reach by Saturday—Greg, who lives in
a two-room stone hut stalked by wild pigs in the midst
of an Ansel Adams landscape, and works as a video art
instructor for mentally disabled adults. Greg is very
sweet, but makes fun of the fact that we own clothing
and objects that were not purchased in thrift stores.

"Just wait," I say. "One day you too will own shoes
and Jockey shorts purchased in retail stores."
I'm assuming that he has indoor plumbing. I could
be wrong.]

Italian tapes

April 1993

Do

fill up tank [so that I don't run out of gas on Santa
  Monica Blvd. again and appear the most pathetic non-
  transvestite on the street.]

wash car and fix taillight [so that I am not stopped
  and searched by LAPD again. And no, Officer, I am not
  going to register my car in California because I
  have not moved here. I'm just visiting, thank you.
  Just visiting.]

start low-fat diet

YMCA

want ads

Daniel—food [Bring him some because he lives in the
  boiler room of our West Hollywood apartment complex and
  needs it, and find out his last name. Also, avoid
  apartment manager because we can't be certain who mur-

dered his sister. And close kitchen windows at night
because when the guy next door is locked out of his
apartment by his roommate and has to crawl up the side
of the building drunk, in his micro-mini sailor-girl
outfit, he screams obscene monologues in Spanglish.]

call police [regarding the car across street with the
Nevada plates that has not been moved in four days,
which I have become fixated on. There's a funny smell
coming from the trunk.]

call Joan's friend re: work

call Will at NY agency for referral

type new résumé

what is Dianetics?

May 1993

<u>Ways to make money?</u>

low-fat cooking for rich people

make soap

make candles

sell therapeutic magnets

pyramid scams

telemarketing

JUMP NAKED
        OUT OF CAKES

learn to drive stick shift [We just bought a little
  pickup truck because our 1974 Plymouth was losing its
  brakes. We were fortunate enough to sell it to a
  demolition derby driver who's gonna paint it canary
  yellow, then hand out sledgehammers to spectators so
  they can beat it to death it for a cable TV audience.]

buy Thomas Guide map [and study it. So that I won't get
  lost. So that when Jim stops the car a few blocks from
  our place, turns to me and says, "I'll bet you have no
  idea where we are," I will.]

call Joe—send pots, TV, stuff from bottom drawer
  [as he is subletting our Brooklyn place and we may be
  here a while.]

get better moisturizer [as this place is a freakin'
  desert and my skin looks like old parchment and feels
  like it should be shed like the top layer of a
  snake's skin.]

thank-you note to agent [for talking about his love
  handles and chocolate addiction and Sandra Bullock's
  star potential. Thank you, Mr. Man in Revlon foundation
  #3 with the floor-to-ceiling wedding portrait of you
  and your horsey, honey-blond wife.]

eat avocados and butter [and screw the low-fat thing,
  as I look like shit.]

buy gin, vermouth, olives [for Dad's martini, which we'll

have ready for him tomorrow when he arrives for a
visit. He's been driving across the country at break-
neck speed and will make it here in a record four
days. He said that he doesn't want to impose, so he'll
just be staying for the afternoon and then it's back
home to New York. We'll convince him to stay the week.]

November 1993

I must read before I get married

The Iliad, Homer
Civilization and Its Discontents, Freud
Don Quixote, Cervantes
Crime and Punishment, Dostoyevsky
Inferno, Dante
Remembrance of Things Past, Proust

January 1994

call Paulie—pick us up? [from airport. From our visit to
    NY and Dad, and Maine and Jim's mother.]

call Leslie, Midge, Marianne [In Maine, Jim asked me
    to marry him...out on a jetty reflecting a full moon.
    It seemed like Earth was the orb in the distance and
    we were on the frozen moon, huddling between rocks,
    and the sound of everything still. I feel thrilled and
    suddenly older, and realize that I've never had any

particular marriage fantasies. No "I always wanted a
ceremony on the beach or a cliff, or a twenty-foot lace
train, or to release two dozen mourning doves." We'll
have a party and round tables and dancing, I suppose.
Yes, a great, fun party.]

call Barbara—YES [Thank you. We would love to have
our wedding at your home that you built with your
strong and able girlfriends in the Maine woods.
Is September good? Is there an old inn nearby for
family and friends? Let's have mussels, berries,
and a band. We can put up a tent in the meadow. But
what about ticks?]

call Dad, Ken, Aunt Jessie, Jim, Sherrie, Greg

Steve—The Rustic?

July 28, 1994

(Mom's birthday)

find humor

have discipline

put fertilizer around the orange tree

smell peaches

light a candle

(July 28, 1994...Mom's birthday)

walk the dog

concentrate on one thing at a time

exercise

eat cheese danish [Mom's favorite]

drive to some "model home" and tour it [in memoriam.
  Like my brother and I did as kids with my folks (when
  we weren't hanging out at their storefront real estate
  office in a strip mall that consisted of a Grand Union
  supermarket, a pharmacy with dusty aspirin bottles,
  and a Chinese takeout joint where we'd get greasy
  shrimp toast and Shar Shu Ding). On a perfect Saturday
  morning we'd drive to some new development, a suburban
  outpost built over the bones of small, extinct marsh
  animals and potato farms. The communities-to-be had
  names like Woodbridge Estates or Framingham Village,
  and we'd tour the model homes, imagining "what if" in
  giant walk-in closets and avocado kitchens. Then we'd
  drive to a diner for Monte Cristo sandwiches, the blue-
  fish special, and chocolate rugelah, then go home.
  My brother puked up his Monte Cristo on the car ride
  back once and hasn't eaten another since.]

August 1994

<u>Do</u>

Buy wedding dress [wedding in three weeks!]

buy earrings

condolence card to Sasha

figure out who forgot to give me $15,000 worth of
   receipts [as I am the wardrobe department accountant on
   a huge-budget Hollywood movie and one of the costumers
   probably spent $500 a yard on some hand-painted import-
   ed silk for one of the stars of the movie who decided
   that it wasn't the right shade of aubergine. I usually
   get the receipts by the end of the day, crumpled up
   like spitballs, pulled from pockets and ashtrays.
   I make notes, cut checks, then report to the Real
   Accountants at the Studio who, I imagine, are beginning
   to suspect that I do not have a degree in anything
   requiring budgetary and pecuniary skills. Hell, I needed a job, an acquaintance in the wardrobe department
   needed to cover her ass, and I was a pink polo shirt
   away from bartending at a Mexican restaurant chain,
   singing the company pledge to the tune of the
   <u>Gilligan's Island</u> theme song. Former accounting
   experience? Yeah, sure, I had experience. I'd cashiered
   part-time at a Chinese restaurant when I was in school.
      At the day's end, at Fortune Gardens Szechuan
   Restaurant I was responsible for rewriting a dozen or
   so of the dinner checks and putting the rest aside for
   a big monthly bonfire. Jackson, the owner, would

explain "Karen-a, the man from the IRS...he very busy
man. He don't have time to look at all checks and
'receeps,' so we gonna make his job easy for him.
Okay?" Wait, here it is. $14,753 to Highland Fabrics
for silk brocade for E's farewell scene.]

call Barbara, Dad, flower lady, band

call photographer guy [he is a friend of a friend who
    lives in northern Maine and is a photojournalist
    specializing in black-and-whites of nature and crime
    scenes. He has agreed to do our wedding pics.]

velvet jacket to cleaners

call Marc and Suz

walk Juno

buy rings

ask Jon to water our tomatoes

finish writing wedding vows

buy AIRPLANE TICKETS

THREE MORE WEEKS TO WEDDING!

September 1994

<u>Groceries</u> (just married)

imported Brie, Romano, feta
Roquefort
dried cherries
chocolate stout beer
key lime torte
Pellegrino water
cabernet
olive rye bread
black forest ham
protein powder
half-and-half
French roast coffee
American Spirits
wild-coriander-scented candles

October 1994

<u>Send</u>

bills!

card to Ken

letter to Aunt Jess

story to AD

résumé to L

writing sample to H

birthday gift to Dad

thank you's to all [for schlepping 3 to 3,000 miles to
    join Jim and me in a small Maine town on the first day
    of sun after two weeks of unseasonable bone-chilling
    nor'easters, even though combat boots (instead of
    stilettos) were required to dance in the marshy meadow.
        Thanks to those who spoke to others after twenty
    years of not speaking, and to those who spoke their own
    inspired words, told funny stories, and read Richard
    Brautigan, scripture, and Dr. Seuss.
        Thanks for the pair of hawks overhead, the sweet
    corn, and song, and berry cobbler, and for driving in
    a pickup truck for six hours with a week-old infant
    to harmonize with those who toted guitars and violins.
        Thank you to Barbara, surrogate mother, planner,
    and the most organized person on the planet.
        And thanks to whomever decorated the porto-potties
    with wildflowers. It was the most fun, most grace-
    filled day I have ever had.]

Jim... thank you

January 1995

<u>To do</u>

pick up work stuff from cleaners [My $800 dress given to
    me by the boutique where I work. My job is as salesgirl
    for $8 an hour—my job that an acquaintance offered me
    after firing her last salesgirl for screaming at an
    indecisive customer. My job—my twenty-second job in
    half as many years.
        On my lunch break I lie on the floor in the
    upstairs dressing room, wool coatdress neatly tucked
    around my body so as not to crease it, and sleep.
    I sleep surrounded by outfits named "Moon," "Gaia,"
    "Frida Kahlo," and "Air." Women stop by to drop
    hundreds on tropical wool sheaths in tangerine and
    charcoal, after lunching at the nearby outdoor cafes.
    I lead them into the fitting rooms and help them dress,
    pushing breasts into bodices and pinning sleeves to be
    altered. I stepped on Bette Midler's freshly manicured
    toes once, showed a stylist shirts that "wouldn't make
    Jennifer Connelly's boobs look so big," accompanied
    some TV actress while she pranced naked up and down
    the bridal gown aisle, tossing dresses into my arms.
    I pretend that I have amnesia and that today will last
    forever so it doesn't matter that the hands on the
    clock don't move. That way, 5 p.m. will be a miracle.]

bring <u>Shipping News</u> to work

bring money for lunch

call Dad [Regale him with exciting Hollywood stories,

like yesterday when the L.A. Bomb Squad cordoned off
the six-block stretch in front of my work because someone left a paper bag of dim sum on a bench and a
passerby thought he heard it ticking.]

write

note to Annie Proulx [My first piece of fan mail ever,
   thanking her for giving me something to read so that I
   don't hang myself with a $400 chiffon scarf.]

call Midge

play lottery

eat arsenic

finish rewrites [although, is the story of a thirty-one-
   year-old Patti Smith–type rock-and-roller who, in lieu
   of suicide, hocks her guitar for a ticket to Alaska to
   help clean up after the Exxon Valdez oil spill what I
   really want to write?]

April 1995

I want

peace
a car less than fifteen years old
a down payment on a house
fearlessness

wisdom
to get up early and write
people to stop assuming that I want to hold babies
to not feel envy
to be Annie Proulx when I grow up

July 1995

<u>I know</u>

On January 5, 1979, Charlie Mingus died at the age of
   fifty-six. In Cuernavaca, Mexico, that same day, fifty-
   six whales beached themselves on a shore.

Healthy wolves do not attack humans.

Leni Riefenstahl <u>knew</u>.

Raymond Chandler didn't write professionally until he was
   forty-five. He didn't even come back to the US until he
   was thirty.

A bullshitter is as likely to mend their ways as a dog is
   to become a Rhodes Scholar.

Maintaining optimism is a habit. Biting nails is a habit.
   Kvetching is a habit. Habits can be made and they can
   be broken.

I must never move to North Dakota, since a group calling
   themselves the Lambs of God are acting like starved,

rabid animals, terrorizing abortion doctors, and threatening their families and children. Lambs do kill.

From the <u>New York Times</u>: Today a Texas man said that his wife's casserole led him to stab a neighbor to death. The man, Mr. Fearance, said he returned home from his job and found that his wife had baked him a casserole with meat. He said he liked his meat separate. "I just snapped," Fearance stated. Then he broke into his neighbor's home and stabbed the man nineteen times.

March 1996

<u>Do</u>

thank you's to Heather, Jon, Bernie [for being so wonderful in my play. Thank you.]

something for Jim

thank Michael [for asking me to do my play, except now he's talking about wanting me to be a giant vagina in a one-act by Tracy and Jon—a five-foot-tall, dancing, singing foam vagina in a play about a woman who loses hers. He says to trust him, that I will be compelling, that no one else can do this. Yeah. Michael could get an insomniac to take speed. Well, I've always wanted to perform under a pseudonym.]

get lawn chairs [for the back of our pickup truck, so that Dad and Ken will have someplace to sit when we pick them up at the airport.]

letter to editor re: <u>W</u> piece [her treatise on touring
as a children's book author, or, more to the point, her
rumination of "I'm just a hometown girl from a small
island called Manhattan and can't imagine how other
nice folks function outside a fifty mile radius of
Lincoln Center or in that dastardly West Coast desert
of glitter-brained zombies called Los Angeles."]

meditate

eat vegetables

talk about motherhood nightmares in therapy

August 1996

Reasons to wait to have a baby

I must first be financially secure

I must first learn to play guitar

I must first learn to speak Italian

I must first have a book published

I must first climb Mt. Whitney

I must first become an amateur kickboxer

I must first have my second book published

I must first become enlightened and
          supremely self-confident

I don't know the first thing about babies

Reasons not to wait

It's getting later

September 1996

<u>Buy</u>

Tony Robbins book

Jon Kabat-Zinn book

Anne Lamott baby book

<u>The Continuum Concept</u>

<u>Blood Meridian</u>, McCarthy

ovulation kit [And have sex with the intent of procreation, which sounds like a felony charge. I've only spent the last fifteen years avoiding getting pregnant, willing every egg to reject visitors, doing every mantra for late periods. It may take a few months to break the news to my body that we are reversing our game plan.]

red wine

dress for Beth's wedding

new notebook

thank you to AD [for publishing my story.]

prescription glasses [Buy them, already.]

October 1996

<u>I must read before I have kids</u>

<u>The Iliad</u>, Homer
<u>Civilization and Its Discontents</u>, Freud
<u>Don Quixote</u>, Cervantes
<u>Crime and Punishment</u>, Dostoyevsky
<u>Inferno</u>, Dante
<u>Remembrance of Things Past</u>, Proust

December 1996

<u>Bring to three-day meditation retreat</u> [in the Catskills,
    over New Year's Eve, where Jim and I are headed,
    instead of getting sloppy, silly drunk and maudlin with
    good friends.]

Pepsi
espresso
coffee maker
comfortable pants
hat, gloves, jacket
pillow
blanket
notebook
wine [just in case]

I must read before I have kids (October 1996)

January 1997

<u>Do</u>

chart ovulation

run

finish <u>Einstein's Dreams</u>

see Tom Stoppard play—Taper

bookstore

drive by [house] listings

call Marion [our broker, and the person most likely to become sovereign ruler of a small country—she's equal parts shrink, staff sergeant, and Dallas Cowboys cheerleader. She affectionately refers to us as "the funky couple wanting a mortgage the size of a car payment." She returns our calls and tirelessly answers our inane questions.]

leave work early

sell artwork [by hip SoHo artist that my brother and I bought as a big investment ten years ago. Unfortunately we would have to kill hip SoHo artist in question in order to increase value of painting. Just get cash. And hope that we both didn't inherit the Rizzo anti-moneymaking gene. My father is a gentle, creative eccentric who worked in advertising when it was a three-martini-lunch career, TV was the technological achievement of the day, and a dove transforming into a bottle of dish soap was a sublime special effect. My mother was a tough cookie who liked anyone who could make her laugh and worked from the time she got out of high school. My brother and I were never for want of anything, but, honestly, the folks never figured out the money/savings/flying not-by-the-seat-of-their-pants thing. It was, indeed, wonderfully romantic that they cashed in their life insurance policies to have a last hurrah together on a Hawaiian island, but it does make me wonder if there is a finance-impaired gene—and if it skips a generation.]

February 1997

Groceries (trying to conceive)

organic beets, carrots, celery, parsley, turnips
free-range chicken
soy milk
organic soy cheese
soy protein powder
matzo ball soup mix
raspberry chi-essence tea
chamomile hawthorn-berry tea
Yogi herb coffee substitute
white rain fertility candles

March 1997

<u>Calls!</u>

IRS [Where is our refund?!]

mortgage company [Lie and tell them money will be in the
  bank by the end of the week.]

credit card companies [and ask them to up our limits.]

Marion [regarding sweet bungalow on the hill with ivy.
  It can't be for real. It isn't a landmark home in the
  shape of Old Mother Hubbard's Shoe, on which one isn't
  allowed to renovate even an eyelet. It's not a house on
  stilts perched on a canyon's edge or one with a Bat
  Pole running from the nursery to the kitchen (which
  could present a problem if I have a child born without
  wings). It can't be. Please let it be.]

April 1997

<u>For my baby</u> (if I ever get pregnant)

Fallingwater, Kaufmann House print, Frank Lloyd Wright
  [because I read that young Frank's mother hung
  architectural drawings in his crib so that he would
  grow up to become an architect—and that wouldn't be
  such a bad thing.]

Charles Addams cartoons [When I was a kid I found a book
  of his cartoons, belonging to my mother, and was so

thrilled at how silly and unfortunate he made grown-ups seem—with their astonished, white-moon faces and the world happening to them in a way they weren't prepared for. It was the same feeling as when I discovered Judy Blume and J. D. Salinger...Hitchcock movies, Woody Allen, Ingrid Bergman, and Cary Grant on the <u>Late Late Show</u>..."Hey Jude," "Goodbye Yellow Brick Road," Stevie Wonder, and the euphoria of sitting in a dark Broadway theater, listening to the overture of a Fosse musical or a Rodgers and Hammerstein revival when I was growing up. Oh. I'm getting so far ahead of myself. Please shoot me if I start waxing nostalgic over Speed Racer and Wild Kingdom.]

Dickens stories

Aaron Copland—"Ballad of Billy the Kid"

David Gray—"Flesh"

Ted Hawkins blues

Edward Gorey sketches

Frank Sinatra ballads

Talking Heads—"Fear of Music"

black clothing

no pastels

no Winnie the Pooh

no commercial merchandise

<u>Masterpiece Theatre</u> poster

July 1997

call fertility doc [re: miscarriage. Dreamt that I had a
body transplant and was living—as me—in someone
else's body. Then one day the woman in whose body I
was living demanded her body back, saying that she
needed it because she had decided to commit suicide.
I tried to explain how unfair it was to me to give up
her body just so she could kill it. I must remain
philosophical. Whoever it was decided at the last
minute that this was not his/her time to come into the
world, that I was not his/her mother, and that he/she
will come back later... again.]

get massage

pack for NY

call Dad, Ken, kennel

find Teenage Fan Club CD

get new notebook

health food store

new ovulation charts

box of fine-tip pens

SIT STILL

October 1997

<u>Find/do</u>

beach for brunch [with Karen, Jim's mother, because <u>she's
  here</u>, in a nearby apartment, fresh from Ohio. Last
  month we told her she was going to be a <u>grandmother</u>.
  That was it. That, the lure of the Pacific Ocean, and
  the fact that Cleveland had seen only forty-seven sunny
  days all year clinched her decision to move. Karen gave
  away her furniture, threw a costume party, burned her
  goddess masks for good luck, and arrived last week with
  a carful of boxes and a new tattoo. Jim hasn't lived
  in the same state as his mother since he was ten. He
  is generous and just a little cautious in describing
  his childhood until then. "Mom was fun, a lot of fun.
  There were surprises and costumes and adventures..."]

find eye doc for Karen

find fridge, sofa—<u>Recycler</u> [for Karen]

<u>Thomas Guide</u>, map of neighborhood [for Karen]

change gyno appt.

edit and type Karen's résumé

Thanksgiving weekend 1997

pack for trip to Sierras [where we are heading to a lodge
    at 7,000 feet with no running water, and will lie back
    and watch icicles form on the porch because I am four
    months pregnant. Jim, with his insatiable appetite for
    all concepts Eastern, Western, psychic, astrological,
    and of quantum physics, read that Sikhs believe that
    the soul enters the unborn fetus on the 120th day after
    conception. Something about that made complete sense to
    us, offering a milestone to mark, an idea for a ritual
    with meaning. So we counted the days from baby-to-be's
    believed conception in July and found it to be the
    day after Thanksgiving. We are going to the mountains
    to celebrate, and Jim is bringing presents for me
    and baby.]

incense

candles

music

boom box

giant fleece clothes

magazines

picnic stuff: pâté, Brie, grape soda, stuffed mushrooms,
    chocolate pie, plates

leash, food, gross giant dinosaur bone for Juno

January 1998

<u>Groceries</u> (six months pregnant)

T-bone steak
filet mignon
Dove bars
soy milk
dill gherkins
sauerkraut
horseradish mustard
organic beets, carrots, celery, parsley, turnips
sour cream
Lay's potato chips
Lipton instant onion soup
Peet's coffee
unscented candles

March 1998

<u>Finish/do before baby Drake arrives</u>

Jim Thompson book

<u>The Stone Diaries</u>

try to fold/unfold stroller [again]

diuretic? [as I've got two O'Doul's, a bottle of black-
   cherry soda, and a glass of H_2O in me. Help! I am a
   Macy's parade float and I'm up here pressed against the

Groceries (January 1998...six months pregnant)

ceiling. I'm a human flotation tank. I yearn to
pee buckets.]

pre-wash baby stuff

assemble crib

buy bumper for crib [and what is that again?]

tweeze eyebrows

bookstore [Research apocalyptic pregnancy dreams,
   Holocaust nightmares, and exercises for leg cramps.]

talk to Dad re: hiring lawyer? [My father's paltry
   savings are down by half and I can't get hold of his
   savvy fucking financial planner guy at Paine Webber
   because, evidently, he's been fired.]

don't worry

talk to Jim re: dining room [The blood-red walls and
   varicose-vein—purple trim looked better on the cover of
   House Beautiful than they do in our dining room. He'll
   understand, even though it took him a week to paint.
   After all, he did mention last night at dinner that he
   felt like he was "sitting in a fucking goth club." He
   is my Martha Stewart hero, scraping and sanding, bound-
   ing up the steps with paint samples, decorating books,
   steaks, caramel apples, and Last Tango in Paris.]

April 17, 1998

I don't know anything (5:30 p.m. ... five hours after
   Drake is born by Cesarean)

It is day, but how can it be the same day as the moment
   before Drake was born?

How could I have given birth in Burbank, across from
   Disney Studios?

Will my organs ever be the same after being lifted out
   and placed on my stomach?

What was the punchline of that Monica Lewinsky joke that
   the surgeon told?

Who does Drake look like? [Jim thinks Marlon Brando.]

Will I ever stop worrying?

Will I ever stop crying?

Will I ever be so full and so empty at the same time?

<u>Do/buy</u>

breast pads [because I am the first mother of the first
   baby in the world and am leaking from every orifice of
   my body, and yes, I know "they are only on loan to
   us," that "they choose us," and that we must "stay out
   of their way and let their true nature reign."
   Whatever. This is my perfect creature whom I MADE and
   I will put in my pocket and run away with and shield
   from the world and eat bark for if I have to. I can't
   stop crying and I can't keep the small throw rug that
   I ordered in the mail because it is stamped "Made in
   Pakistan," and I can only imagine the small hands of
   weary, underage children weaving late into the night,
   foregoing school to bring me this rug. The rug is going
   back in the morning. I cancel my mail order catalogues
   and cry some more. Then I press my lips to my son's
   furry head, close my eyes for one moment too long, and
   nearly keel over in a narcoleptic instant. Life is
   good. Time to change my pads.]

flame-proof fireplace

send thank you's

send announcements

what is insurance deductible?

return phone calls [while Drake naps. Or not. Or brush my
   teeth. Or read. Or sit and stare at the spiderwebs
   forming in the orange tree.]

call Doc [Ask if my organs will stop feeling as though they are crashing together like passengers on a crowded subway at a sudden stop.]

August 1998

Buy

baby development book? [so that I know what other parents are talking about. Conversation with the father of a four-month-old as he hovers over his baby's carriage in the mall:

>Me: Oh, look. She's found her thumb.
>Him: Yes, she just recently crossed the vertical meridian with her left hand and found her right to bring it to her mouth. She's been a little disoriented by her discovery, but she's right where she should be.

I tell him I understand, but don't really. Will my generation's kids be truly fucked up?]

dental floss

teeth whitener [I dreamt that two government agents knocked out all my teeth, causing my lips to cave in. I made Jim buy me a set of wax candy teeth. Then Jim and I escaped on a train, where I gave birth to quintuplets. We asked Rosie O'Donnell, who was a passenger on the train, to babysit the day-old infants for a short while. When we got back, she told us that the oldest quint had tried to kill the other babies, and she thought that it would be best if we killed him before he succeeded. We agreed, and buried him under a floorboard.]

postpartum book

Lancôme reconstructive cream—big tub

Kwan Yin—goddess of compassion—book?

Devas, angels book? [Up in the Sierras for Jim's birthday last month; snow still on the peaks, cold winds at night while we slept in our cabin. Drake is nestled in his bassinet in flannel feeties and blankets, a wool cap pulled snugly over his head—the kind of cap that takes three hands to pull on: two to tug each side over ears, one to hold a tiny wobbly neck.

In the middle of the night I woke to check on Drake. He was sound asleep, still wrapped except for the cap. Not wanting to wake him, I scrunched the cap between the side of the bassinet and his head. In the morning, the cap was on his head. No, Jim didn't wake all night.]

baby sleep book [Ken called this morning and asked how I was doing. I said, "I'm up every two hours, I haven't had a full REM cycle of sleep in four months, and I'm having nightmares." He said, "I can kind of relate. My cat gets me up a lot during the night." If he had been in the same room with me I would have pulled out his tonsils.]

November 1998

notice up at Pasadena City College [I am losing memory of
    myself as woman outside of house. I must find someone to
    come in a few hours each week and watch the boy, some
    Nice Young Woman who likes kids and is studying to be a
    teacher and who doesn't have a mental illness. Hmm.
    That car outside the house looks suspicious. Now I'm
    imagining Nice Young Woman running out the front door
    with Drake screaming in her arms, to a waiting, beat-up
    Buick revving its engine, driven by Swarthy Unshaven
    Man. I jump on the hood of the car. I scream. Nice Young
    Woman appears on <u>America's Most Wanted</u>. I wish Drake
    would wake up.]

call Bernadette, Midge... girls' night out? [Dreamt that
    Jim and I needed to leave Drake with Bernadette for a
    couple days. As I was driving to Bernie's house, Drake
    became a tea bag and fell into the crack between the
    front seats of the car. We were unable to retrieve him.]

buy new humidifier

solid finger food

lead test on tub

best butt exercises?

memory exercises?

have date

have sex

December 1998

For Drake

Barney

Silly Zoo Songs

Raffi in concert

Prokofiev

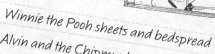

Winnie the Pooh sheets and bedspread

Alvin and the Chipmunks sing '80s rock

powder blue sleepsuits

pale yellow onesies

lime green overalls

Tickle Me Elmo and his freaky giggling friends

Take down <u>Masterpiece Theatre</u> poster
[It makes Drake cry.]

January 1999

<u>I know</u>

the "self" is overrated

"should have's" suck

sometimes after a pot of coffee I can get a glimpse of my higher power

868-0529, my phone number when I was ten

MA3-6579, Sue's phone number when we were ten

I see Lincoln Navigators as deadly tanks and instantly dislike the drivers

I have too much information at my fingertips

When I have a moment of extreme peace, I imagine the two main characters in <u>The Unbearable Lightness of Being</u>, when they reach a peace and happiness that will never be surpassed... and then they die

We have plenty. I want more.

Alfred Eisenstaedt took photos until he died at ninety-six

(I think) the very cute, freshly scrubbed twenty-two-year-old at the Gap counter was flirting with my still-postpartum size-12 self

April 1999

<u>Today</u>!

get Drake birthday party stuff

cake stuff

kiddie pool and toys

dinosaur stuff

call Madda [What to get for one-year-old?]

Jim——Greg called [He's tired of making beer and minimum wages and wants to know if he and his master's degree should move to Los Angeles, Hawaii, or North Dakota. North Dakota? Maybe I'm making that up.]

call computer guy [My computer has caught a nasty, insidious virus that has obliterated only my annotation files. Annotating movies is a freelance job of mine, as in:

Dialogue: "I'm not playing patsy with you, you motherfucker."

Then I explain: i.e., "I won't let you take advantage of me in this volatile situation;" "patsy" is slang for "person easily taken advantage of"; "motherfucker" is vulgar slang for "despicable person."

I do this so that "get a taste of your own medi-cine" doesn't wind up being translated into Swahili as "ingest your own prescription drug." And so that <u>Small Time Crooks</u> isn't translated into Chinese as "Little

Things I have actually (and unfortunately) said to my child this week (July 1999)

Bent Tools" and "<u>Sugar and Spice</u>" isn't touted as
"<u>Condiments, the Movie!</u>"

When I'm annotating a movie, I spend a lot of
time talking to myself. Some days I like to speak only
in ways needing annotation. Like yesterday when Drake
and I were at our favorite park and a movie was being
filmed nearby. A woman wearing headphones and a sour
expression approached us. "We're shooting a movie here.
How would you two like to be extras?" she asked, unable
to conceal her contempt for having to recruit mother-
kid combos.

"How would you like to wash my laundry on a rock
by the side of a stream?" I answered.

With this latest computer virus I realize that
I'm tired of explaining what other people say.
Perhaps it was then that the great good goddess of
freelancing winked at me. In the immortal words
of Albert Einstein, when he spoke for the first time,
"The soup is too hot."]

shower

July 1999

<u>Things I have actually</u> (and unfortunately) <u>said to my
child this week</u>

You can't sit naked on Mommy's face.
I don't want you eating food with your feet.
Please don't put your finger in your butt.
Please don't drink out of the dog bowl.

You can't have my beer.
Mommy needs to poop without your help.
Can we please just have a grown-up conversation?

November 1999

<u>Do and stuff</u>

Jim's Aikido demo downtown [Jim is devoted to his Aikido
  practice. That is, he chooses to be thrown across a
  padded room by other black belts in the spirit of some
  strict feudal Japanese boot camp—he chooses twisted
  knees, welts, and shoulder sprains to rid himself of
  his acting angst in lieu of heavy drinking. That is a
  good thing, I remind myself.]

buy nice stationery

Jim—Greg called [Greg chose Los Angeles and now lives a
  mile away. Can he stay with us for a few days? Greg
  wants to know. He doesn't feel safe in his apartment
  because his next-door neighbor, newly out on parole,
  threatened to kill Greg's dogs if they dig up the guy's
  petunias again.]

drumming lessons?

Teenage Fan Club CD

Tai Chi?

make GIFT/CARD LIST!

buy Yerba Mate—online [It's tea; some dark, earthy
   tea that Argentinean cowboys drank for sustenance and
   occasional psychic awakenings. Jim must replace his
   Columbian coffee with it because his pupil isn't
   dilating. "Not to worry," said his GP, "but let's have
   you see an ophthalmologist," who said, "Not to worry,
   but let's have you see a neurologist," who said, "Not
   to worry, it's probably not a brain tumor but we're
   gonna take you off coffee, chocolate, and red wine."
      What? What?! Jim believes that the six darkest
   steps of the day are from the bed to the coffee maker.
   And if there is no red wine, what is the point of
   6:30—8:00 p.m.? No chocolate reward...What then is
   the point of protein, steamed vegetables, and complex
   carbs? What, may I ask?]

organize closets

January 2000

get vomit smell out of car

preggers clothes to Goodwill

eat beets

ignore M—IGNORE

buy goldfish?

ring-around-the-rosy [Teach it to Drake because yesterday
    he and I watched as a mother and her two toddlers mer-
    rily spun themselves dizzy in the sandbox singing it.
        "What they doin'?" Drake asked.
        "Oh, shit," I thought, "I forgot to teach my kid
    ring-around-the-freakin'-rosy."]

Wendi to babysit??? [so we can go to <u>Jitney</u>, the August
    Wilson play. How does he write like that? August.
    What a great name. If we ever have another kid, a boy,
    we should name him that... or Chance or Wynn.]

accept own lack of ambition

April 2000

<u>Groceries</u> (Drake is two)

organic squash, sweet potatoes, and peas
organic free-range chicken
organic soy chocolate chip wheat-free cookies
organic fruit-sweetened oat cereal
multigrain gluten-free bread
unsweetened juice, soy milk
tofu (silky)
Amy's organic lactose-free whole wheat mac and cheese
organic coffee
birthday candles

parent workshop at Drake's school [What is that?]

silent auction committee? [What is that?]

trash committee [What is that?]

recycling committee? [Of course.]

read school handbook

snack stuff for Drake's class [We are starting at a
nursery school co-op. I'm snack parent tomorrow, which
means that I work in the class and provide a tasty,
healthy snack. Should I splurge on organic? Does water-
melon have any nutritional value? Grapes are too
dangerous; mozzarella sticks, dangerous too. No razor-
edged chips, no peanut products... and what about the
lactose-intolerant girl on my class list? Will the kids
like me... I mean, will the parents? Will I like them?
I hope I don't cry. Drake won't cry. Did I buy the
right size Tupperware container for his cubby? Have I
lost my fucking mind? Aunt Jessie told me that she
started a nursery school co-op in Hempstead, Long
Island, when her boys were toddlers. She said that she
and my uncle went to Jones Beach at night to fill a
pickup truck of sand for the sandbox. At least I don't
have to steal sand. I should be grateful for that.]

last draft L.A. Times piece

recommendation letter for Ken [as he is applying for a

mentorship program at some Lower East Side halfway house. Jim's been a "Big Brother" for years, and it's made a difference for him and his "Little Brother," who is now twenty-one. Ken is a kind, sympathetic guy and will make a wonderful mentor. That's what I'll say. And that he has excellent taste in shirts.]

call Midge, Steve, Marianne

registration and immunization records

find new pediatrician?

call Karen—when shrink? [As in, what time is her shrink appointment, which Jim and I have been asked to attend? Karen has a job, an acupuncturist, a therapist, a psychiatrist, and a reason to call daily. I know more about her psychic, emotional, and physical history than my own mother's. But I only have to picture her and Drake making cookies or watching a <u>Little Rascals</u> video together, Drake in a bat mask and gold lamé cape, and I'm grateful that she's here. Karen keeps a bin of toys for Drake, toys duplicating those of my husband's childhood, toys that she's scoured thrift shops and garage sales for, toys scrubbed up with an eye or wheel replaced and voila! like new! She is Drake's Nana, barely older than my mother was when I was in high school.

    I knew my mother's mother. She was the only grand-parent left when I was born. I knew her only as the stern old woman in a yellow housecoat whose passion was farmer cheese. I found out recently that she'd been depressed for much of her life. "Probably

clinically depressed," is how my aunt put it (I can
hear my mother, "Who knew?"). Jim remembers <u>his</u> grandma
"Doodcakes." He remembers her syrupy apple pies and
rock-solid gallon-size tubs of vanilla ice cream.
He remembers her sitting on the linoleum floor playing
marbles with him; remembers the circular patterns
of her gentle back-scratches.

    Drake knows back-scratches like that. They come
with a pink powder puff that Karen pats on his neck
and shoulders after a bath or after he's played
with her collection of toys and costumes.

    "Hey, buddy," I say to Drake, "you know how lucky
you are to have Nana?" <u>You're</u> <u>very</u> <u>lucky</u>.]

December 2000

send mortgage payment [the mortgage on my house,
    our house. Got a house and a mortgage and a husband,
a baby, a dog, and a nice neighborhood. Am I that
different than the girl who walked home to her place
on 10th Avenue in Hell's Kitchen with a pocketful of
tips, clutching a corkscrew for safety? If I got
home before eleven and ran up the five flights to my
apartment, I could catch Terry Kinney walking home
after a performance of <u>Orphans</u>. He wore a long trench
coat and always walked down the middle of the street.

    Am I so different than the girl in Williamsburg,
Brooklyn, keeping warm with Jim under old sleeping bags
and a grandma quilt? Could hear the J, M, and Z trains
from bed; people living, running, shouting outside the
window. So cold in winter, the radiator pipes banging,

and a cab cost twelve bucks from Times Square. Who
would I be if I weren't a mother? Who would I be if
I were single? Who would I be if I'd been wildly rich
and successful at an early age, or... if I hadn't
backed out of that three-day EST seminar, offering me
the chance to rid my life of the caca and neuroses
preventing me from success and self-fulfillment when I
was twenty-two?]

get back to therapy?

shower

get a haircut

call Leslie, Marianne

call Midge [tell her I get the Bad Mommy Award
  for today.]

finish Mother's Day piece [But can I say in that magazine, "Mom admitted years later that she was scared to
  death to move from Manhattan to the suburbs because she
  thought all the women would be hanging out at their
  back fences talking about the consistency of their
  kids' shit"?]

Drake to park [but not the one where some mother
  invariably asks me how many words my kid knows, or
  what language he's learning in his morning preschool,
  because _her_ three-year-old is learning French and
  performing <u>King Lear</u> at his. And what kind of flash
  cards do they use at my son's school? Flash cards?

My son ate the flash cards he got from a well-intentioned friend of mine, and what he didn't eat, he glued to the carpet.

First things first. My son is learning important concepts like that red paint mixed with the blue glue makes a viscous yellow gel that remains yellow even when stuck to brown hair. Also, red paint doubles as toe polish because "it's more beautiful to paint the whole toe, not just the tiny little nails."]

box books for Salvation Army [the 358 "raising baby" books by assorted aspiring Dr. Spocks and Spockinas, which I will never read.]

May 2001

New York Post!!! [Find a copy somewhere. Ken just called. Evidently the twenty-one-year-old that he was mentoring—whom he had dined with and had over to his apartment—helped dismember a man in the Bronx. Cops don't think that Ken's mentee (is that a word?) is the killer, only the dismemberer. I told my brother that perhaps he had some good influence on the kid after all. Ken hung up on me.]

wash Juno

pack earthquake bag for Drake

buy digital camera?

magazine proposal to Joy ["An American Muslim Woman in Jersey." Who are these mysterious women I see laughing amongst themselves at the mall, with their princess statures, black scarves, and Doc Martens? Interview Pam... my friend Pam, Heather Locklear look-alike, former Irish Catholic Jersey girl, now happily married to a Muslim man and mother to three whip-smart kids. Ask her who else I could talk to.]

baby and mom yoga?

megavitamins

Tracy

blood work, vitamins

Marc on <u>Rosie</u>! 3:00 p.m.—tape show

learn Italian

September 11, 2001, 3:00 P.M.

shower

call Jim [again. If airlines still not operating by night, tell him to just rent a car and drive home and charge it to the production company.]

gyno asap [because I am pregnant and want to make sure that all this shaking and sobbing is not affecting the tiny girl in my belly. How can this small person absorb the grief of a swollen grown-up body? Will the collective sadness creep into her cocoon? How can I be having a baby now? I whisper desperate apologies to her when, abruptly, I have a surge of clarity in my weary hormonal brain. Whoever my daughter is, she's choosing to come at this particular time. She knows what she's getting herself into. She will be who she is supposed to be, despite me. New or old soul, she will be sad or happy or introspective or combative, not because of my choosing. She is coming prepared. Who knows—maybe she's returning after a hundred years' absence; maybe she's come back after being gone just a day. The fact is that she's choosing to come into this place, in this mother, at this time... with something to teach me.]

bookstore with Drake [even though this is his twenty-ninth day dressed as Spider-Man and he won't take off the costume, and why should he, and why should he think that today is different from any other day because, after all, he is only three?]

do not turn on radio or TV [when Drake is awake.]

make calls

e-mails

make playdate [but not with little K, whose psycho mother thinks that a three-year-old needs know that airplanes can fly into buildings.]

October 2001

<u>I want</u>

a new Volvo with airbags and sidebags and optional
helmets for children under twenty-one

Drake to ride his bicycle only in pastoral park settings,
and learn to swim expertly by the time he is four, and
become a black belt in karate so that he may always
be able to defend himself, and to wear a bulletproof
vest if he decides to travel abroad, and to have great
intuitive powers so that he will always be warned in
advance of possible harm. I want him to grow up in a
city so that he will be street-smart and savvy, as much
as I want him to grow up in a small town in Maine so
that he will remain innocent and be golden brown in the
summer. I want him to be liked and never teased
and accepted and happy and self-sufficient and wise and
able to find humor and realize another's pain and be
sympathetic, generous, successful, loved, and able to
leap tall buildings in a single bound.

to stop having awful dreams

to finish my magazine article about optimism

November 2001

send chocolates to LB

reply to e-mails re: <u>Salon</u> piece

be here now

run fast

shower

listen to Sarah Vaughan without doing anything else

write proposal for piece on Mom

resole boots

find video of <u>How the Grinch Stole Christmas</u> [not the
   Jim Carrey debacle, but the one I waited to watch each
   year as a kid, with Salisbury steak TV dinners and
   Creamsicles. I tell Drake that I'm going to find this
   "special video of the book." I tell him that my mom
   took my brother and me to Aunt Jessie's house to watch
   <u>The Grinch</u> because they had a color TV and we didn't
   (until 1973). I tell him how it was my favorite show.
   He listens with interest, then asks, "Did they have
   cars when you were little? But there weren't any airplanes, right?"]

Third week in January 2002

Get done

Dad to neurologist [for follow-up Alzheimer's test, which
  he will fail again if the doctor asks him what city he
  lives in. Dad is here, in an apartment a mile from us,
  because Ken and Jim and I finally convinced him to move
  from his solitary place at the tip of Long Island.
  Sometimes when my father gets in my car, though, I lose
  my place in time for just a moment, and I think that
  I'm eight and my son is my brother and we're just
  waiting for Mom to join us. Is that what's meant by
  time running parallel? Does anyone else ever have that
  feeling? Should I be taking more supplements? Could
  I possibly get by in a day without a list? More precisely, how old is too young for Alzheimer's?]

finish article

pack a suitcase

make copies of all Dad's keys

talk to Dad's super re: broken bathroom tile

pick up lab tests (Dad's and mine!)

b-day gift for Drake's party

pay parking ticket!

give birth [preferably Thursday]

January 31, 2002

<u>in my head</u> (an hour after August's birth) [I am
  alone, thank God, swaddled like a big baby after
  this C-section, alone with my thoughts before starting
  the next eighteen years. The doctors all disappeared
  down the hall with Jim holding August. She swallowed
  meconium and our blood pressures dropped dangerously
  low before the birth, but she is going to be fine,
  tiny, perfect creature that she is. A friend of a
  friend, who labored for sixteen hours before giving
  birth by C-section, still rails against the "evil
  paternalistic doctors" who conspired to slice her open
  and rip out her baby, her <u>healthy</u> baby, which would
  have been <u>something</u> <u>else</u> otherwise. But she's still in
  therapy about it; about being robbed of her "ultimate
  life-affirming experience" (isn't that the part where
  the baby comes out alive?), still drawing crayon pictures of red flames surging from torn flesh. Hell, I
  wish I could have squatted next to a tree with only a
  rag between clenched teeth and given birth. Maybe I did
  that in another life. Oh. Now I'm giggling. Now I'm
  crying...again. I am so out of my mind with joy.
  And worry.]

remember sound of August [There is nothing like the sound
  of a baby announcing itself as it enters the world.
  There are so many people in the room. Then, abruptly—
  magically—there is one more.]

Drake [has wanted a baby brother or sister since he could
  say it.]

Jim [I dug my nails into his hands so hard I thought I'd touch bone. He didn't flinch. I asked him to take a look at my organs laid out over my stomach. He wouldn't, for fear of fainting. Damn, I'm crying again.]

May 2002, 4:00 A.M.

living will [Add Ken as guardian]

oil change

batteries in fire alarms

Ziploc bags

look up photos of black widow spiders and poisonous indigenous plants

snake bite antidote kit

review CPR book

November 2002

<u>Do</u>

Finish <u>FP</u> article

bring Dad to doctor [with Drake and August, and hope that
the doc will let Drake play with the electrocardiogram
machine again.]

Dad's dentist appt.——new dentures

Drake's doc appt.

write never-to-be-sent letter to mag [for killing my
piece in the eleventh hour. Then frost hair, grow out
mustache, wear little white anklets with tennis shoes
and high-waisted shorts, and just concentrate on being
the perfect mother.]

Target list

grocery list

buy online X-mas gifts

finish Drake's applications [to private schools because
the public schools in my area boast one teacher to
thirty kids, with supplies enough for half that. So
we're applying for a home equity loan, thinking posi-
tive thoughts, and opting for private school——<u>liberal</u>
schools offering pacifist leanings, the lyrics to Bob
Dylan songs, not-so-subtle vegetarian pleas, spare the

cow and boycott McDonald's essays, "War is not healthy for children and other living things" slogans, diversity, and noncompetitive ideals—schools offering all that will insure that my child is totally unprepared for the real world. I must finish my application. If only I were a single Native American Buddhist nun with a law degree and a Romanian baby, I'd have a better shot of getting him into my first choice. But no, the best I have to offer is my suburban, middle-class, Jewish/Italian background and a gay mother-in-law who, one time when off her lithium, told me that I wore combat boots in order to "keep weighted to this planet and not float away," then proceeded to sprinkle me with bone ash and gray goose feathers from her shaman's bag.]

baby SLEEP book [because I
    haven't been sleeping
    and I'm gonna have
    a nervous breakdown
    if I don't get
    a solid four
    hours soon.]

tea—NO COFFEE!!

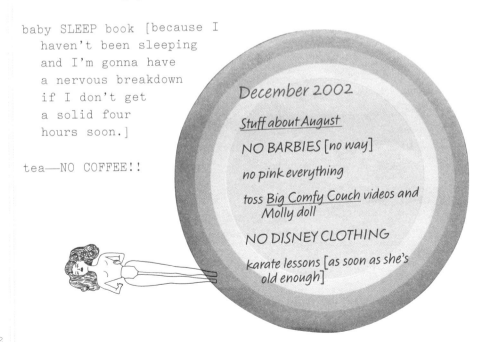

December 2002

Stuff about August

NO BARBIES [no way]

no pink everything

toss Big Comfy Couch videos and
    Molly doll

NO DISNEY CLOTHING

karate lessons [as soon as she's
    old enough]

January 2003

no adverbs other than "said" [says Elmore Leonard]

financial aid apps. due

copies of tax returns

biomedic cleanser, superhydrating moisturizer

tithe [UNICEF?]

babysitter for August [That would be Wendi, Patron Saint
  of Children Who Question Relentlessly and Eat Only
  Beige Foods.]

time?—Drake's school tour [Our final one, thank God. Last
  school tour we were one of thirty pathetically eager,
  yearning-to-be-judged well-adjusted yet attractively
  eccentric, enthusiastic yet reservedly cool, parents.
  Our parent tour guide said to us, with enough smugness
  to imply that she had three genius children at the
  school, "So, why do you want your child to go here?"
      I was weary and developing carpal tunnel from all
  the pages of lovingly handwritten and not-so-lovingly
  rewritten application essays. "I don't know," I wanted
  to say. "Your school has the best fucking monkey bars."
  Instead, I launched into an impressive imitation of a
  woman who might actually have read about Piaget and
  John Dewey. Then they took my son, and six other kids,
  into a room for two hours to be judged objectively by
  teachers with clipboards and solemn faces. Drake told
  me that he ate bagels and dressed up as a ballerina.

I suppose that's one way to weed out potential psycho-
pathic cream cheese—smearing cross-dressers.]

Dig out ELO, Pink Floyd, and Elvis Costello albums
   for Drake

Abbott and Costello videos

thank you to Jules [... soon to be sister-in-law, for the
   haircut, for the X-mas gifts, for dinner, for saying
   "yes" to my brother.]

copy of will to Jim's dad

have sex [But tell Jim it's not sexy when he pretends
   to be other people before we do it. Although, "Vince
   the Mechanic" is kind of fun.]

April 2003

DO LEG LIFTS

remember Drake as an infant

remember Dad with Mom

remember August's baby smell

remember myself rested

cut toenails

learn to fence

call Jessie [I just found my baby book, a faded pink silk
    binder titled <u>Best & Co: A Record of Baby's First Year</u>.
    I was thrilled, as I never imagined my mother stopping
    long enough to make one. Finally, the detailed record
    of my "firsts" and my mother's keen observations of
    "the beginning of me." Page one: there was a photo
    of Dad carefully cut into an oval shape, and a picture
    of me with a New York Infirmary sign on my blanket.
    Next page: under "messages, flowers, and gifts," my
    mother had listed all the people who had come to
    visit...Grandma Sonkin, Les and Lee Tomalin, Mac and
    Irene, Winnie and Dick...and so forth.
    On the third page: under "First Day," <u>my</u> first day,
    a <u>list</u>:
        8 oz. Carnation
        16 oz. water
        2 $\frac{1}{2}$ oz. sugar
    Then, dated two months later:
        13 oz. Carnation
        17 oz. water
        4 oz. sugar
        cereal
        vegetable (no peas or beans)
        fruit (plain)
        1 oz. OJ
    This. <u>This</u> I read in the fourth combined year of
    breast-feeding two kids of my own. I'm calling Aunt
    Jessie to find out if Mom really just fed me the
    equivalent of liquid Twinkies and a multivitamin after
    my birth. Not that it matters. I just want to know.
    Why? I don't know. It doesn't matter. Forget it.]

airline [Change return flight from the twenty-first to
the fifteenth]

call Ken [Dad got sick, suddenly jaundiced and puking.
Jim rushed him to the emergency room. He can't make it
to the wedding. He may not make it, period....Don't
tell Ken that. His doctor says that he needs surgery
immediately. How immediately, I ask? "We've scheduled
him for tomorrow at three p.m. We have a surgeon, but
if you have someone else in mind..."
　　Sure, I just happen to know a few oncologist
surgeons specializing in gastrointestinal cancers. I'll
interview them immediately and weed out the one who's
killed the fewest patients. This is not happening.
This not happening—is happening too fast. "No, we'll
go with your person. I'll be there in the morning."]

call Jessie [Tell her what's happening.]

call Midge, Karen [Yes, it would be great if you'd check
in on Dad while we're at the wedding.]

finish wedding speech

Jim re: poem?

talk to Dad [Explain, gently.]

Third week of September 2003

Drake art supplies

when is the party? [for Drake to meet his
    kindergarten class.]

call Dad's landlord [Let go of his apartment.]

sell big furniture

box up Dad's personal stuff

ship statues to Ken

call Ken and Jules re: airport Thurs. [Remember to ask
    them about their honeymoon first.]

move Dad [into our house. Because the cancer in his
    gut is going to kill him much sooner than the early
    Alzheimer's. Just months ago he was playing golf,
    climbing after Drake on a jungle gym, chasing after
    August at the beach, laughing madly until they both
    collapsed in the sand. While he is lucid, we talk to
    him about tubes... for food... for breath. We talk about
    resuscitation. He grunts disgustedly at the notion of
    being kept alive by artificial means. We all agree on
    hospice at our house. Then Dad asks for a whiskey and
    a slice of pizza.]

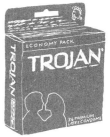

Drugstore stuff (October 2003)

October 2003

Drugstore stuff

straws

pacifiers

Tampax

morphine

Corona Light

brown liner pencil [for Jim... to darken his white eyebrows... for an audition. He's the TV guest "psycho,
bad cop, abusive husband, pyromaniac," and the man who
sits with my father nightly, he with his Corona, my
father with his morphine cocktail as they watch the
evening news. Yesterday Jim came into the living room
dressed in pressed chinos, a baby-blue oxford, and
white sneakers. "There," Jim said, "How do I look?"

"What are you?" I asked.

"Social worker, but he winds up being the killer.
Killer, but he's a social worker."

"I don't know. It's too... clean. Maybe a
darker shirt."

Drake comes in. "What's your audition, Dad?"

"I'm a social worker."

"Nah, that's all wrong. You're supposed to have on
a black shirt and black tie and black shoes. Like Cobra
Bubbles—in <u>Lilo and Stitch</u>? He's a social worker and
that's what he wears, Dad."

August runs into the room and eyes Jim suspiciously. "Hey, baby," he says to her, holding out stiff cotton arms.

"No like, Daddy."

My father comes in. "Is everything all right?" He gestures to Jim. "Hey there... young man. Have you got... one of those things where you do that thing... you do?"

"An audition."

"Right. Go knock 'em dead." Dad throws a few air punches, nearly knocking himself out. "Give 'em hell. Who... are you supposed to... be?"

"I don't know anymore, Tony. Maybe you should tell me."

Dad squints. "Is this a trick question?"]

toothpaste

shaving cream

diapers

aspirin

Depends [for Dad. I hope the cashier doesn't think they're for me. No, she won't, of course she won't. I'll mention that I have a toddler. I'll wear lipstick and smile and look like a woman who has control of her bladder. The cashier won't give a shit.]

gummy bears

condoms

November 2003

Get/do

find espresso machine [and USE IT.]

get Clash CDs [because I miss hearing them.]

buy StryVectin [because it promises to make my skin look
ten years younger and had fucking better because it's
as expensive as gold bullion.]

rent The Misfits [because I'm PMSing and I can only deal
with watching a movie in which all the actors have been
dead for years.]

read Peter De Vries [because he's darkly funny and dead.]

talk to Dad about dying [Dad has forgotten his diagnosis
and plans to move to Arizona when he gets better. A
house in the mountains maybe. Or in Lake Havasu, where
the London Bridge is. We can all move there and Jim
can commute...to Los Angeles. He asks why he's feeling
so lousy, and we remind him that he's very sick. "How
sick?" he asks. Sick like when Mom was sick and you
took care of her, I tell him. "But I've never been
sick before," he says, incredulous. That's how I want
to go, is what I want to say. Not sick for eighty-some
years, then, boom, I've got six months.
    "I don't know, Dad."
    "But how did this happen?" He insists. "I can't say
my feelings. Tell me, is my mind going bad or is my
body really sick?"

What's the right combination of truth and hope?
"I don't know," I mumble.
"We're in...the sunny land...west. You know."
"Yes, California."
"I am so...unknowledge...of what goes on in
the whole area. How...is...Jim's father?" He asks, to
show me that he remembers Jim, remembers Jim's
dad, remembers.
"He's fine."
"How old is he?"
"He's sixty-one. Jim's dad is sixty-one."
My father looks aghast. "Is that possible?"
"Maybe he had Jim when he was thirteen," I say.
"Are you playing with me?" he asks, looking pained.
"Oh, no, no. I'm just kidding, Dad. I'm kidding."
Then we both stare at the floor.]

RSVP for Dina's cocktail party [Cocktail. Had a friend
who camped out at our house last week doing odd painting jobs for us. He'd sit with Dad on breaks, listening
to Dad's stories and silence. His last day here he said
to me, "You know Karen, we could have a party for
Tony. Have your family and close friends and...have a
cocktail. We could have music and we'd all stay into
the night, however long it took."

Hmm. A party...That's not a bad idea—while Dad
still has the energy. With cocktails. Dad loves a good
Beefeater martini. "Yeah, that's not a bad idea," I
say. "A cocktail party."

"Right," my friend says. Then very slowly, "I know
how to get that cocktail. It would be very peaceful.
And we'd all stay...until the very end."

Hmm. I'm a little confused. Then, abruptly, I'm

not. "Oh. Oh, oh! You mean a <u>cocktail</u>, like a <u>final</u> cocktail. Like the-last-cocktail-he'll-ever drink cocktail. Oh! Oh, well, thanks. Yeah, um, let me think about it and I'll get back to you. But thanks." We're not having a cocktail party.]

Drake ready for kata test?

December 2003

<u>Gifts to buy</u>

Drake, August, Jim

Teachers—school, karate

Jim and Sherrie—John Prine CD, boater things?, photo album of kids!

Karen, Ken, Jules

kid parties

Dad [What to get for the man who'll likely be dead in two months, who wasn't supposed to make it till Christmas, who appears abruptly, like an apparition, in the doorways of my house, emaciated, one foot in the next world, asking, "Is there anything I can do for you?" What to get for the man who would never want sympathy, ask for help, or admit to growing old. I know what my son wants for Christmas. He wants to take his grampa to

school for show-and-tell after he dies. I tell him that
there's probably a rule against bringing dead people
to school. He's gonna check with his teachers anyway.
<u>I</u> <u>should</u> <u>call</u> <u>Drake's</u> <u>teachers</u> <u>and</u> <u>warn</u> <u>them</u> <u>that</u> <u>Drake</u>
<u>will</u> <u>ask</u>.]

First week, January 2004, 4:10 A.M.

<u>Buy</u>

condolence cards for Aunt Jess and cousins [There's been
a rash of old guys dying. Uncle Joe, my new sister-in-
law's father, the husband of my mother's oldest friend,
Uncle Mort... Dad is next and I haven't asked all the
questions, haven't gotten all the answers. Who were my
parents long ago? Where did they come from? What did
they want? Did they find what they were looking for?
The details they divulged about their Lives-Before-Me
were presented in abrupt burps... footnotes without
introduction or end.... The Great Depression wasn't
good, but everyone did the best they could. When my
teen-age mother was working at Manhattan's Stage Door
Canteen, she saw Don Ameche pick his nose. Dad crash-

landed in a B-52 during a test run and the goddamn
army dentist pulled out and replaced most of his teeth.
Mom worked for the head of Revlon in the '50s and
drove a gold MGB midget ("with a stick shift...the
only way to really drive"). Dad directed a little civil
defense film called <u>Duck and Cover</u> that instructed kids
to dive under their desks or fly off their bicycles in
the event of an atomic blast. My parents had kids late.
"You and your brother came along. What else do you need
to know?" I forgot to ask about who I was as a child.
Was I smart? Was I weird? Who will know if my son is
like me when I was five? I am too late.
Shitshitshitshitshit.]

batteries

new smoke detectors

college fund

biohazard suits for kids [Search Web. Just in case.]

Call throat doc—tell him he's a moron [Today Dad was
   convinced there was something lodged in his throat and
   insisted on seeing a doctor. His GP said to humor him,
   and sent him off with Jim to see a throat doctor who,
   evidently, had no fucking clue as to what hospice
   means. He told Jim that Dad was terribly undernourished
   (no shit) and that death by starvation was a terrible
   way to die. Oh my God, what have we done? We called
   Cyn, our hospice nurse, and told her everything. I
   heard her yell to someone, "You won't believe what this
   asshole doctor said to my people."

We are her people and she is ours. She heaves herself up our steep front steps and stands, panting at our front door, at first twice, then three times weekly, now daily. "You don't have any more steps in there, do ya?" she greeted us on her first day. She is the last in a line of hospice nurses assigned to us, nurses dwarfing Dad by two and three times. As Dad got smaller, they came larger.

Cyn returned to the phone. "Those fucking, excuse me, doctors," she sighed. "Doesn't he know what hospice is?"

"It's Dad's body closing down, right? Isn't that what's happening... supposed to happen? He didn't want feeding... all the tubes and—"

"Of course!" She said. "You're right! I'm so sorry. That doctor... well, he was just plain wrong. I'm sorry. Damn doctor."

I threw together a milkshake, unable to swallow myself, and brought it out to my father. "Dad, please, you've got to drink this."

He looked at me, it seemed with pity, and said hoarsely, "Honey. I'm just not hungry."]

End of January, 2004

August birthday party stuff

new dress for August

Ken—what time at LAX?

bake cake? buy it?

go to bank [and change my PIN... my PIN of twelve
years... because I can't freakin' remember it.]

go through Dad's strongbox [Dad has fallen... no,
slipped... no, leaned into a coma. One minute sitting
on his own next to me on the couch, the next minute
falling, or rather, leaning in against me and into a
coma. The hospice nurse and I picked him up and laid
him in bed, his being caught in this petrified body;
caught, waiting for release, for the vessel to shut
down and the portals to open. My father told me that
he believed in God, and although I did find some
ancient, mildewed Bible among his belongings, I never
actually knew him to have set foot in a church. My
mother was Jewish and they were married by a justice of
the peace. Hospice sent chaplains in the beginning, but
Dad danced around their inquiries into his faith, his
simple and very private faith. He believed in the here
and now, in what he could touch and feel and do, and
he believed in those he loved.]

call Jim's folks

February 14, 2004

pick up undertakers' gloves [that they left in the driveway. By the way, they really do arrive in dark suits even at four in the morning.]

call Dad's brothers

call Aunt Jessie

e-mail people

call hospital equip. rental place [pick up bed, mattress, commode.]

call crematorium [When will Dad's ashes be ready? Do I pick them up? Do I need an appointment? Do I get to pick out the urn? Is there an urn catalogue?]

call Cyn [our hospice nurse, who came even though she wasn't on duty because I didn't want to wait with anyone else at in the middle of the night for the undertakers. As she collected all Dad's meds and dumped them in the toilet, she said, "This all the morphine? I just have to ask."

A few weeks before, sure that we'd done everything wrong for Dad, I'd asked Cyn how she could do this. "I mean, all your patients die."

"Oh, hell," she said, "anyone can deliver a baby. Been there, done that. But to give a person a good death, to help them with their final wishes... that's something. This is something."]

March 2004

<u>Do</u>

lunch with Nicole!

mammogram

<u>Mary Poppins</u>

birthday gift——Drake's party

frame picture of Dad and seagulls

letter to Uncle Dan

call Aunt Jess

send thank you's

grocery list

letter to hospice nurses

contact Conelrad.com [which is campaigning to get <u>Duck and Cover</u> inducted into the Library of Congress National Film Registry (alongside <u>Schindler's List</u>!). Evidently that little civil defense movie was one of the most watched educational films, if not <u>the</u> most naïve and paranoia-inducing, ever made. They want to interview Dad, its director. Isn't timing everything?]

walk [I've been thinking of Dad's walk when I do——his

brisk, torso-straight, not-missing-a-beat, grateful-to-be-doing-it-again walk. I relax my shoulders and become aware of my feet rolling off the ground with each step. I've never thought of my father's walk so precisely till now. Is that what happens—our parents become more a part of us when they die? Or is it that we never actually stop and examine the small idiosyncratic gestures that made up their lives until those lives are over? I'm certainly more my mother now than when she was alive. She was fond of saying, "The first hundred years are always the hardest." Of course, I'd roll my eyes at her. Now I can't wait to say it to my kids so that they can roll their eyes at <u>me</u>. I can only imagine how like my father I may become.]

April 2004

<u>bring to mountains</u> [Going to spread Dad's ashes because that's what he wanted: part of him at 8,000 feet, part in his gravesite—with a view—beside Mom.]

coats, hats

hiking shoes

teaspoon, tablespoon, serving spoon, plastic spoons [decide which to use later]

urn

snacks

water

poem

photo of Dad

camera

map

change of clothes [in case the kids spill Dad
  on themselves]

tissues

Dad's favorite Chianti

May 2004

<u>Groceries</u> (Drake is six, August is two)

Pringles
Oreos
peanut butter
American cheese
Kraft macaroni and cheese
Froot Loops
organic apple juice
organic sugar-free gummy bears
mayonnaise
vanilla ice cream

green tea, black tea
coffee
wine (red, white)
citronella candles
(bum one American Spirit Light from red-headed
  checkout guy)

June 2004

answer the telephone! [Otherwise my kids will grow up
  thinking that you have to hear who's calling in order
  to decide whether or not to answer the phone. When I
  was a kid we had one of the first answering machines.
  It was the size of a backpack and my mother let it
  pick up calls at the end of the day. "Don't touch the
  phone," she'd yell. "The squawker will pick up!" When
  she'd get home it was, "Let's see who's called on the
  idiot box."]

playdates!

ice-skating schedule

Drake to dentist!

bathing suits

floaty arm things

Drake haircut?

Jim—Greg called [He can't babysit on Saturday and, boy, are the kids gonna be disappointed. He swings them upside down after taking them out for burgers, ice cream, and sunset hikes. Uncle Greggy is sorry, but he has to work another sixty-hour week editing The Starlet, then meet with an architect to discuss an addition to his house.]

ask Wendi babysit Friday night? [Wendi told me, almost apologetically, that she senses Dad in the house some-times. She tells him "It's all right. Drake and August are fine and safe and happy." I'm envious of her sixth sense and vow to listen more carefully to the shadows.]

get plane tickets for Joe's wedding [and our first weekend without kids, with Marc and Suz, whose first weekend it was also sans kids. Weeha! Gonna stay up all night with old friends, sleep in, listen to music, drink beer in honky tonk Memphis bars, bum cigarettes. Oh. Wait. I can't leave the kids... Wait... What if—
    I'm reminded that when Barb and Frank travel to NYC without kids, they worriedly go on separate planes... in case of extreme tragedy. My friend in Italy with the sweet, funny husband and two beautiful kids worries so hard that she can make herself pass out.
    Me, I've always stored in my memory the specifics of particular tragedies—those recent, historic, acci-dental, and intentional. I've imagined the people involved and what they could have felt. A cupboard of tragedy that I open and rearrange every so often to remember what's there, and to put life's small daily traumas in perspective. Every day I hit that fork in the road. One way involves fear and anxiety, and the

other involves—now, let me get this right—faith, is
it? Or trust, or some sort of surrender? My internal
map instinctively chooses "Route Fucking Anxiety Sixty-
Six." And I work to change course. Every day.]

September 2004

<u>I know</u>

my kids teach me more than I teach them

everyone has an insane relative

everyone has a story

everyone is in pain

gossip is bad and I love it

TV newscasters should not look like porn stars

people who run red lights while talking on cell phones
   should be publicly flogged

cars should not be big enough to carry entire soccer teams

big ponies are for experienced riders

1994/2004

Why I Hate L.A. (1994)

it's always fucking sunny

I never get to wear a coat

I have to drive everywhere

everything is outdoors

IT'S ALWAYS SUNNY

it's not New York

Why I like L.A. (2004)

it's sunny

the kids don't need coats

I can drive anywhere

everything is outdoors

it's not New York

October 2004

<u>eBay stuff</u>

list throne chair [which was in damn good condition until
the idiot movers hauled it here from New York with the
same care and enthusiasm reserved for roadkill and
political prisoners. It was also left out in the rain
one night because we were busy moving the dozen boxes
of my father's tchotchkes, rock collections, <u>Reader's
Digests</u>, and iron statuettes that recently came into my
possession. But the upholstery and wood detail are
still very nice. The chair belonged to my mother, who
left it to my father, who carted it around for eighteen
years until I inherited it. My mother had this chair
reupholstered in the 1970s, but I don't remember anyone
actually sitting in it. And let's face it, <u>my</u> unwanted
stuff is <u>your</u> found treasure, which seems only fair
because <u>my</u> house is furnished with the restored and
repainted junk that used to be in <u>your</u> house.

I'm selling it because, quite frankly, I've no room
for even another damn Matchbox car, and I have a fear
of excess stuff. I don't want my kids to have to haul
out my broken and obsolete treasures after I die, only
to be displayed on the folding tables of yet another
depressing LA estate sale. Yes, I have fond memories
of the throne, but, honestly, I have twenty-seven other
things a fraction of its size that hold the same
nostalgia for me. I won't subject this chair to ship-
ping, so come and get it or send someone gentle for
it. Peace and no reserve.]

find Indian costume and headdress

ninja costume w/ sword—bid!

fairy princess costume

pink tiara and wings

Fan travel trailer??? [Jim has been watching it on eBay
   for six and a half days. He's serious. He wants to tow
   a little vintage trailer for us all to camp in. He
   imagines technology-free weekend adventures to remote
   forests, the kids making memories that they'll treasure
   for a lifetime. He won't win it. It's nearly over our
   sniper budget. The owner's not gonna pull his fifty-
   year-old trailer from freakin' Wisconsin. The thing
   sleeps four if you count the kid-size pantry over the
   stove. It is cute though—original birch interior and
   all-flat aluminum exterior curving down over flat
   sides, looking like a giant ham can. It needs polish-
   ing, new tires, and a fridge. Oh, crap.]

November 2004

<u>What Drake believes</u>

we need to adopt a baby

that Luke Skywalker should have joined the Dark side,
   if only to be with his dad

a person can die from being too sad because their heart
   can break

he needs an "outfit" for meetings, school, and birthdays

he is going to marry his sister (but not at a place where
they throw rice at you)

people on commercials who tell you stuff that isn't true
are bullies and should be punished

spirits are actually very tiny when you see them floating
above your bed

soldiers should enter a city and say to the people,
"I mean you no harm"

people should use water guns so no one gets killed

December 2004

Must read

The Iliad, Homer
Civilization and Its Discontents, Freud
Don Quixote, Cervantes
Crime and Punishment, Dostoyevsky
Inferno, Dante
Remembrance of Things Past, Proust

January 2005

<u>Do</u>

prep writing samples

Ivan—congrats [for getting into Brown!]

Conelrad—congrats [<u>Duck and Cover</u> is inducted into the
  Library of Congress National Film Registry.]

put pics in photo album! [especially since my folks
  stopped putting pictures in albums around 1974, leaving
  me with a Chianti crate full of hundreds of orphaned
  photos of people and places I don't remember, honeymoon
  poses mixed in with my birthday parties, Ken's baby
  pictures back to back with a strange couple at a '40s
  ski lodge. I will leave that crate to my kids and they
  can sort it out after I'm gone.]

call Doc back—no refills [Nice of him to call and ask
  if I wanted refills for the drugs he prescribed after
  I pulled a back muscle at the gym and passed out from
  the pain. Fell right neat between the bench press and
  free weights. My emergency room doctor was fatherly
  and concerned, gave me muscle relaxants, painkillers
  and Vicodin. And, oh, that Vicodin! Very nice, thank
  you, but no thanks. Although I did put a few aside for
  a rainy day. I can see how you could get used to it.]

drumming?

Tracy—visit me

Drake and August—send thank-you card to Nana [Thank you
   for Drake's Spider-Man backpack, August's jacket, and
   the photo album of you in your new community on the
   other side of the country, which you ran off to in the
   middle of the night four months ago. "Tell me again why
   Nana left," Drake says.
      "Well, Nana loves you and August very much and...
   but...she...wasn't happy enough here...and...well...
   we couldn't make her happy."
      Drake thinks about this for a moment, then says,
   "I think Nana wanted to live with us. Maybe she can
   have August's room if she ever comes back."]

January 2005

Questions for trailer guy [Our twelve-
   foot, 1959 canned ham is on its way
   from Wisconsin.]

propane tanks—how to fill? [And how safe?]

heater working? [And how safe?]

pantry for kids to sleep [And how safe?]

mountain travel? [How safe?]

how to hook to car?

AstroTurf included?

<u>August's wish list for her third birthday</u>

shiny pink shirt and pink corduroy jeans

pink unicorn

pink pony

another Barbie [The first five were handed down from
   Barb's daughters, who took pity on August for not having any. And since Barbies multiply when left naked in
   bathtubs overnight, at last count we were home to
   eleven naked Barbies—two without heads. August wants
   flannel feety pajamas and modest pink nightgowns for
   them, but there is no such thing. They must sleep in
   their sequined wedding gowns and leopard hotpants. One
   of them is battery-driven on skates and ends up grind-
   ing against a table leg like some freakish Masturbation
   Barbie. "Look, Mama, she's dancing!"
       This reminds me that everything is a matter of
   perspective. Curiously enough, August is very wary
   of her lone Ken doll, keeping him naked in his own
   plastic box, separate from the Barbies. Mostly she's
   disappointed that he has no penis. "Boys are supposed
   to have penises, Mama. If they don't, they're girls."
   (Toymakers, take note.) Another Barbie will probably
   materialize overnight, and in the morning we will find
   her floating facedown in the bath.]

pink pajamas for Barbie and a purple robe and shoes

Ariel and Cinderella nightgowns [Disney. Sigh.]

find <u>Big Comfy Couch</u> videos and Molly doll on Ebay

start ballet lessons

February 2005

<u>Shopping</u>

sneakers and sandals for Drake

new <u>gi</u>

supplies for sea creature project

new phone [that gets freakin' reception in the back of
the house.]

notebook

fun Drake lunchbox snacks

return flower-girl dress

clothes for August [Bring her shopping with me. She won't
wear a thing if she hasn't picked it out herself. She's
three, and she has her own taste and style. It only
took me twenty years to find mine. When I was in fourth
grade and needing my first pair of bellbottom jeans, I
remember pleading with my mother before she headed off

to Orbach's department store, "Please, Mom, they gotta be Wranglers or Levi's and please, please get them in the boys' department. And Mom, <u>blue</u>. <u>Blue</u> jeans." Mom came home with "flared" (as she called them) denim pants with florescent green, yellow, and orange zodiac signs on them. I didn't want to hurt her feelings. "Mom, they're... really nice but they're not <u>really</u> bellbottoms. I mean, the bottoms have to be wider and they gotta be long enough so you step on them when you walk. They're nice, but didn't they have just plain blue?"

"Sure they did," my mother said, "but with these you won't see yourself coming and going. Everybody'll be wearing 'just blue' and you don't want them so long that you trip on them. Pretty groovy, huh, kiddo?" Yeah, yeah, zodiac signs are good, Ma. Groovy.]

March 2005

<u>What is necessary</u> (not necessarily in this order)

coffee

exercise

sex

delicious food

peaceful surroundings

friends

satisfaction

surprises

no surprises

health

disappointment

sorrow

silly rhymes

new music

old music

chocolate

gratitude

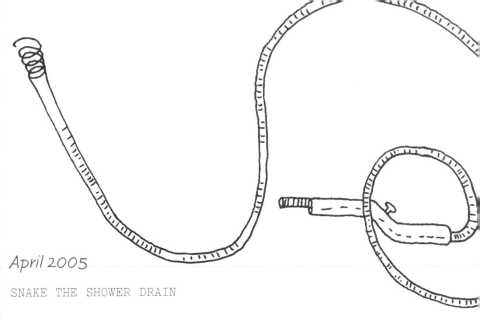

April 2005

SNAKE THE SHOWER DRAIN

get lecithin, omega-3, extra B-complex [to try and remedy
  my premenstrual insanity.
          "Mom, I love you," Drake says.
          To which I respond, "Oh, God, I love you, too...
love you so much I—I—"
          "Mom, are you gonna cry?"
          "Probably. See, I'm only as happy as you are happy,
as well as you are well, as safe as you are—"
          "Okay, Mom. So can August and I eat marshmallows?"
          I'm reminded of when my brother and I were in our
teens and, unbeknownst to us, Mom was entering
menopause. She was crying at red lights and threatening
to mow down the Waldbaum's produce manager in the
parking lot for calling her "honey." Who knew?]

balance checkbook

WALK!!!

Drake playdate

check lottery #s

tiki lights and bark cloth curtains for trailer

schedule snack parents

eat some meat

send thank you to C [for having the grace to telephone me
   personally to tell me that the magazine was killing my
   piece. I can do that, be thankful, now that I have
   "distance." And not because I rolled up all the back
   issues I had of the magazine into fireplace logs and
   toasted marshmallows over them. When my kids came home
   with my husband, as I was sitting on the sofa, staring
   out, wiping my swollen eyes after finding out the shit-
   ty, surprising news, my son asked "Why's Mom so sad?"
   To which Jim replied, "Well...Mom's sad because...
   because she thought something was going to happen...
   and it didn't."
      And if that doesn't remind me of my total lack of
   control in this absurd comedy of errors, and that to
   anticipate anything is a man-made joke, then I don't
   know what does. Oh, boy, have I learned a lesson....
   Oh, yeah. Now excuse me while I go and make the same
   mistake over...and over...and over again.]

May 2005

<u>What August needs for a trip to the post office</u>

Kola [an imaginary friend]

Keenu [an imaginary friend]

Aleya [an imaginary friend]

Minou [an imaginary friend]

Little Pete [a two-foot-tall boy doll in a hard hat and tool belt]

Slema [the Barbie who is "sick and throwing up"]

Tama [the non-puking Barbie]

water

sandals

a hat

a snack

ballet slippers

bathing suit

June 2005

BRING TO BEACH

sensitive kids SPF-30 lotion

SPF-15 lotion

water-resistant sunscreen

Jim's stuff

Motrin, Red Bull, herb tea

lip balm

Thich Nhat Hanh book [But if I'm reading this then how can I truly "be" at the beach?]

Life of Pi [which I will never get to.]

Enquirer, Star, People ... stop and buy [which I will get to.]

sand toys, bulldozer

Frisbee, kite, boogie board

umbrella

kids' wet suits

hats, blanket, sweatshirts

Bring to beach (June 2005)

pretzels, cut fruit, raisins, PowerBars, bananas,
    Pringles, sandwiches

water, juice boxes

baby powder

water shoes

change of clothes for everyone

July 2005

Get/do

George Plimpton book [Just got back from working out at
    the Y. Feeling strong, pumped; lifted those ten-pound
    dumbbells like 'dey was lollipops. Oh, yeah! I've
    figured it out. I'm gonna be the forty-something-woman-
    with-kids version of George Plimpton. Gonna challenge
    myself. Gonna take risks and write about them. Oh,
    yeah! Only... I'm scared to death of getting punched in
    the nose. I don't like heights... or airplanes... or
    amusement park attractions for riders over forty-two
    inches high, and I seldom want or need to travel out
    of a ten-mile radius. I always imagine the worst-case
    scenario. Maybe I'll learn to fence, or I'll ask Greg's
    fiancée to teach me to ride a motorcycle. Maybe not.
    Maybe I'll just take a nap.]

talk to Kurt re: bathroom [Kurt, our handyman/actor, who,

at six-foot-seven, towers over the entire family and is usually covered in white plaster-dust. He yells into his cell phone to his agent, then runs off for one-line commercial auditions. "Hey, Drake, August. When I get back I'll give you both sledgehammers and you can help me knock down this wall!" Sure, Kurt.

The kids love him, regaling him with streaming monologues which Kurt pretends to understand, when, actually, he is too high up to hear half of what they say. They like that he talks to our house and his power tools. Not "talks," exactly. "Don't do this to me!" he screams at a piece of molding that doesn't fit neatly, or "Son of a bitch! Where the hell are you?!" at a misplaced drill. Jim reassured our ninety-eight-year-old neighbor that he wasn't the one with the Tourettic outbursts, and that no one was being beaten.

Our bathroom floor is sagging and something is leaking water under the tiles. Hopefully Kurt can come on Friday. He takes his iced tea sweet and coffee light with sugar. Then Mike the plumber will squeeze us in and tell Jim to just get a huminybummer, attach it to the spiglywatt, so that the whoosymama doesn't go bust again. Jim will listen politely then remind him, "Shit, Mike. My dad sold ladies' swimwear and called a plumber when a doorknob needed tightening. You lost me." Mike'll smile in pity because we don't have _real_ jobs, then round up the goddamn stuff to fix the toilet himself.]

Talk to Jim re: Drake's bike gear [Drake: Mom, tell me a story about when you were a kid.
Me: Let's see...in summertime, I'd be out at night riding my bike in the dark with my fr—

        Drake: What?! What were you doing out in the dark?
        Me: Well, my folks were probably relaxing on the
porch with a drink and a cigarette—
        Drake: A cigarette?! Are you kidding?! Didn't they
know they could <u>die</u> from that?!
        Me: Anyway... I remember riding over this huge bump in
the street—
        Drake: You were riding in the <u>street</u>?!
        Me: So... I scraped my knee from—
        Drake: You didn't have on your knee pads?!
        Me: Well, no... okay, we didn't—
        Drake: Did you have on your helmet?
        Me: (Sigh.) We didn't have helmets.
        Drake considers this for a minute, then, "Mom, how
'bout I just enjoy myself today and not wear any stuff?"]

Jessie—when to visit?

Geri—when baby due?

Paulie and Madda—when back to Italy?

August to dentist

plan Jim's birthday

call Winnie—<u>great</u> <u>story</u>!

call Bernadette re: dinner [She will come to <u>my</u> house, as
    always, armed with Cabernet and chocolate and patience.
    We'll down juice glasses of wine as she follows me from
    kids' dinner to bubble baths to beddybye, while we have
    hit-and-run conversations in triple time. I can't wait.]

Last week in August 2005

<u>Get/do</u>

where is my check from magazine?!

Jim's Aikido demo

chiropractor appt.

is crown covered on dental???

wedding gift—Greg and Alli!

file reference stuff [Those articles I cut out in May
  about all the great, free, educational summertime
  happenings for kids in and around LA—articles about
  how summer is a time for kids to learn new hobbies,
  attend workshops on dinosaurs/identifying indigenous
  plants/vegan baking, a time to hear free music under
  the stars. Well, we didn't do any of it. Nope, not
  MOCA or the free jazz or 1960s pop or the African
  drumming or the traditional Appalachian folk dancing at
  the Pavilion. We did blow up an oversized kiddie pool,
  and encouraged use of the dozen cheap water pistols and
  floaty things designed for a small ocean. I tried to
  remember to drain the damn pool every few days, but
  I'd forget. Now our backyard, with several large rec-
  tangular patches of seared, dead grass, resembles an
  alien landing pad. We ate too many cheap blue-and-pink
  Popsicles, and on days when it was too hot to lift one
  foot in front of the other we took refuge in movie
  theaters and ice cream parlors. I think that mostly
  the kids had fun. I sure hope so.]

call Jim's folks

have kids call Karen?

pitch idea for piece to <u>V</u> editor

pack trailer [Yes, our trailer, accessorized with vintage
  candy-striped awning, four matching lawn chairs, and
  AstroTurf. Drake loves his private sleeping loft,
  and August likes scrunching up next to me on the twin-
  sized foam mattress. Jim lowers the table and converts
  the dining nook into a bed. The chance to build roaring
  campfires has brought out the pyromania in my kids,
  and they thrill to walk to an outhouse in the dead of
  night with flashlights... They're even more thrilled to
  pee in the woods. Sometimes, though, the going is
  a little less rustic and we find ourselves nestled
  between behemoth trailers hauling expensive motocross
  bikes, Jet Skis, kayaks, and small cars. Guys in crew
  cuts or thinning mullets play Jethro Tull and ZZ Top.
  I heard someone fiddling with a stereo until, "Lionel
  Richie, yes!"]

August 2005

<u>I know what is inherited</u>

eye color
hair color
bone structure
tendency toward insanity

obesity

dimples

thighs

cancer

orgasms [which is more information than I ever needed
    to know.]

September 2005

<u>I want</u>

happiness

truth

patience

a nice piece of seared tuna

an espresso served correctly with lemon rind

a movement to eliminate the terms "multitasking" and
    "at this point in time" from the English language

something fun for the whole family to do

naps

a day during which I don't lose my keys, a library book,
    an earring, my wallet, a lipstick, my grocery list, my
    reading glasses, my son's memos from school, my temper,
    or my humor

First week of September 2005

money to Habitat for Humanity!!!

call Ken [You're getting divorced?!]

Leslie—when play opens?

increase home equity line [Otherwise Jim may follow Marc's suggestion to chainsaw bears out of logs for a living. Maybe we should move to Maine, open a little luncheon joint, and name the sandwiches after dead actors.]

get Drake school stuff

find red shoes

get ballet tights, leotard

e-mail new families re: work days

post potluck sign-up sheet

Drake lessons—violin? guitar?

talk to Jim re: monkey mom ["So-and-so's a bully," Drake said yesterday. To which I gave my pat liberal reply: "Babe, he's not a bully. He probably just needs someone to be nice to him or listen—"

"Mom!" Drake said, holding his head. "Why do mothers always say that? Why can't you just believe me? I know you had bullies when you were a kid. What did your mom say when you told her? I bet she also said nooo, <u>he's</u> <u>not</u> <u>a</u> <u>bully</u>."

He's right and I tell him so. Then I offer, "Drake, when I was a kid, Mark Waters used to wipe his feet on my favorite velvet coat on the bus ride home. I had to get off at the first stop, a long way from my house, just to get away from him. And I'd cry." I stop and reconsider. "But he wasn't really a bad kid, he was just——"

"Oh, my God, Mom! Why do moms have to say 'he's not really a bad kid'? Moms have been saying that since they were monkey people. One monkey mom told her kid that, and then that monkey mom told her kid. When I'm a dad, I'm gonna stop it."

<u>Fucked</u> <u>up</u> <u>again</u>. "Drake, you're right. I'm going to stop it now."

"Dad, too?"

"Yes. Dad will not be a monkey mom."

"Admit it, Mom, when your mom said that to you, didn't it make you mad?"

"Yes. Yes, it did Drake. Yes, because all I wanted her to do was go to Mark's house and kick his butt."

Drake smiles and we have, for a moment, reached an understanding. Just for a moment. Even though I don't normally advocate kicking child butt.]

Today, in the early morning quiet, while August and I ate grapes and Mike and Ikes, I asked her what she wants to be when she grows up. She gave me a list.

<u>I wanna</u>:

be big
have hair

be a ballerina
do karate
have baby costumes
be a tiger
and be a woman—a happy woman, like you, Mom [And
   herein lies one of those tiny windows of pure,
   unadulterated...what...? Calm? Relief? Being? One of
   those moments in which, if one could choose, one
   would live forever. And abruptly the "other" thoughts
   bleed into it—a replay of the nightly news, of
   suffering in a country where no one visits, do we
   have the mortgage, what of the old-growth trees, is
   this ache in my throat happiness? They're delicate,
   those moments of—dare I say it—joy. Often too brief
   to recognize and always a challenge to maintain.
   But, hey, out of the mouths of babes... A happy
   woman...like me. Who knew? Which reminds me...

buy:

Mutant Ninja toothpaste
colored Band-Aids
ibuprofen
tiramisu
learn Italian CD

Acknowledgments

Supreme gratitude to my mother and father who were never not proud of me, and to my brother, Ken, who picked up where they left off.

At Stewart, Tabori & Chang, thank you to Jennifer Levesque, my editor, for realizing _Things to Bring_ . . . in a way that I'd only imagined, and to woolypear and Peter Arkle, for their creative vision (and patience). A world of thanks to Andrea Glickson and Claire Greenspan (not least of which was for getting me out of the house), and, especially, to Leslie Stoker for getting behind my dream experience with her incredible workforce of publishing pros.

To my agent, Joy Tutela, for her stubborn belief that I had this book in me and her uncompromising guidance in making it happen, grazie mille.

Gratitude for years of encouragement and humor (and for reading all my s#!t) to writers and artists Leslie Ayvazian, Nicole Gregory, Bernadette Sullivan, Tracy Poust, Marianne Larson, and Margaret Hussey. Special thanks to Marc and Susan Parent for their kick-butt wisdom and cheers on this particular journey.

Thanks to Kaldi, Buster's, and The Coffee Table coffee shops (where much of this book was written) for not kicking me out after hours spent at a time with only a lone cup of coffee.

To all the folks in this book, thank you, goodnight, pleasant dreams, sleep tight, you, too, whatever you say.

etc.

Editor: Jennifer Levesque
Designer: woolypear
Production Managers: Kim Tyner and Anet Sirna-Bruder

Library of Congress Cataloging-in-Publication Data
Rizzo, Karen.
   Things to bring, s#!t to do ... and other inventories of anxiety : my
life in lists / by Karen Rizzo.
        p. cm.
   ISBN-13: 978-1-58479-542-1
   ISBN-10: 1-58479-542-5
   1. Women—Time management. 2.   Lists—Miscellanea. 3.   Rizzo, Karen.
I. Title.
HQ1221.R59 2006
305.40973'09045—dc22
2006012417

Text copyright © 2006 by Karen Rizzo
Illustrations copyright © 2006 by Peter Arkle
Excerpt on page 11 copyright © 1934 by Ogden Nash, renewed.
   Reprinted by permission of Curtis Brown, Ltd.

Published in 2006 by Stewart, Tabori & Chang
An imprint of Harry N. Abrams, Inc.

The text of this book was composed in Typewriter Elite and Calliope

Printed and bound in the United States of America
10 9 8 7 6 5 4 3 2 1

HNA
harry n. abrams, inc.
a subsidiary of La Martinière Groupe

115 West 18th Street
New York, NY 10011
www.hnabooks.com